Contents

Introduction

Dermot A. Lane

It could be argued that Religion, Education and the Law are the three pillars of civilisation. Indeed, anyone vaguely familiar with history will be struck by the recurring reference to the centrality of Religion, Education and the Law and to the constructive tensions between them over the centuries. The great danger to-day is that the vital contribution of religion will be removed from the dialogue with education and the law.

Over the weekend of 29-30 November 1991 Mater Dei Institute of Education hosted a symposium open to the public on the general theme of *Religion, Education and the Constitution*. The occasion of the symposium was twofold.

In the first place, Mater Dei Institute was celebrating its Silver Jubilee of involvement in teacher education. As a College of Education concerned with the professional formation of Religious Educators and teachers of other subjects for post-primary schools, it was considered appropriate to engage in an analysis and reflection on some of the issues relating to the work of the Institute over the last 25 years. In the second place, the Institute had hoped that the symposium would coincide with the publication of the Green Paper relating to the proposed Education Act and thereby provide a forum for the public discussion of some of the contents of the Green Paper. For various reasons outside our control, this latter hope could not be realised. In retrospect, the non-appearance of the Green Paper was something of a *felix culpa* because it freed the speakers to devote themselves without distraction to their specific areas. The happy result is four papers which stand up in

4

their own right. At the same time, it is hoped that the publication of this collection of essays will provide a context for and background to public discussion of the Green Paper, when it does appear.

Down through the centuries, different philosophers such as Plato, Augustine, Aquinas, Buber and Gadamer have promoted an understanding of human enquiry in terms of dialogue and on-going conversation. Each of these philosophers in his own way has shown that what is most essential to our humanity is the capacity to engage in dialogue with others, to take seriously the questions of others and to be enriched – not threatened – by that which is different. The purpose of the Mater Dei symposium in November 1991, and now the publication of the papers, is to promote an open dialogue on some of the issues relating to the relationship between Religion, Education and the Constitution. The spirit of the dialogue envisaged is one which seeks to go beyond the confines of victors and vanquished. Genuine dialogue enriches all the participants because it is based on a respect for the views of all and a willingness to accommodate as well as a desire to promote clarification and the transformation of participants in the shared search for truth. When the dialogue breaks down, then there are only losers.

A PREVIEW OF PAPERS

Turning next to the individual essays, in the opening paper on 'Religion and Education in a Pluralist Society', John M. Hull begins by noting a resurgence of interest in Religious Education throughout Europe. In the first part, he talks about Religious Education as learning religion, learning about religion and learning from religion. Concentrating on the latter, he highlights some of the difficulties experienced in England in maintaining a balance between Christianity and other religions, as required by the 1988 Education Act.

In the second section he outlines the role of Religious Education as a critique of religion. Religion is an ambiguous phenomenon and for that reason needs to be subjected to critique. Particular attention should be paid to the critique of ideologies, including the ideologies implicit in religion. In this regard, he focuses on the role of Religious Education as an emancipatory discipline, with a capacity to liberate adults and children from oppressive aspects of religion. At the same time, Religious Education can also open up the treasures of religion.

In the third part of the essay, Hull develops an understanding of Religious Education as a gift to human development. If Religious Education is to be acknowledged as a gift to human development, then it must be recognised that it is possible for religion to be true or false. True religion promotes genuine dignity, autonomy and communion of human beings and in this sense becomes a gift to human development.

In the fourth part of the essay, Hull outlines the role of Religious Education as Christian mission. The mission of Christian Religious Education is to serve humanity and not merely to propagate itself. This emphasis he traces back to Jesus and in doing so warns against a supplanting view of Christian Religious Education vis-à-vis other religions. Poignantly, he sums up his own vision of Religious Education as a movement 'out of pain into pain'. Religious Education should seek 'to enable young people and adults to be delivered from their own personal pain and to shoulder the pain of the world.' To refuse pain is to promote an impure understanding of religion. Hull concludes his essay by looking at the mission of Religious Education in England and Ireland.

Kevin Williams, in his paper on 'Usefulness and Liberal Learning', notes that one of the fears of educators is that the spirit of the proposed Education Act in Ireland will endorse the current tendency to promote a fashionable and superficial notion of economic usefulness as an educational aim. The argument of the first part of the essay is that a vibrant productive economy does not require a direct relationship between the school curriculum and the world of work. The attempt to promote economic productivity directly through the curriculum is misguided because employment opportunities are related to the state of the economy rather than to the character of the educational system.

The principal argument of the second part of the essay draws attention to a paradox in the notion of liberal learning – namely, that it is through a curriculum of such learning that the school best prepares young people for the world of work. In spite of fashionable demands for 'relevance' in the school curriculum, evidence continues to confirm that what employers value most highly is a general education, together with the skills of accurate and effective communication and appropriate personal qualities.

Williams argues that it is through the curriculum of liberal learning that we best serve the human and practical needs of our young people. Before equipping young people with vocational skills, we must foster in them an ability to make considered choices. In order to respond constructively to programmes of vocational training, young people need an education which endows them with a vision of the worthwhile in human life. And it is a curriculum of liberal learning which will enable young people to develop this vision.

In the concluding section of his essay, Williams looks briefly at the role of Religious Education within the curriculum of liberal learning. In its sensitivity to the dignity and preciousness of the human person, Religious Education has a unique potential to help young people to live more fully and more richly. The knowledge and understanding acquired in other subjects can be drawn together in religion class to enable students to develop a holistic vision of life. Religious Education is therefore not only consistent with the essential purposes of liberal learning but no subject is more likely to contribute to the humane, spiritual and civilising purposes which characterise the pursuit of such learning.

In 'Irish Educational Policy in a Philosophical perspective: The Legacy of Liberalism', Eoin Cassidy examines the relative neglect of an explicit philosophy of education. He connects this neglect with the pervasive influence of certain forms of liberalism on education.

His essay outlines some of the negative features of liberalism and their effect on education. These features include the 'belief that truth is ahistorical', the emergence of a competitive individualism and the influence of pragmatism. He shows how the aims of education as stated in recent policy documents have been shaped mainly by a philosophy of Western liberal individualism. As a result of this influence, there is an absence of reference to the importance of dialogue, solidarity, the transformation of the world and social justice as well as a reduction of the classical notion of excellence to that of instrumental efficiency.

To overcome the prominence of particular expressions of liberalism in education, he suggests a series of counterbalancing moves. These embrace an emphasis on the interpersonal dimension of human nature rather than the merely individualistic, the recovery of cultural memory within tradition to balance scientific positivism and a retrieval of commitment to the classical idea of excellence to overcome pragmatism. He concludes his paper by outlining a theory of excellence that goes back to the Greeks and explains what he means by the importance of keeping alive the cultural memories enshrined within tradition for a philosophy of education in Ireland to-day.

In the final paper, 'Education and the Constitution', Gerry Whyte examines the power of the State to prescribe a minimum standard of education, the obligation on the State to provide for primary education and, lastly, the possible constitutional implications for State financing of denominational education. He points out that judicial precedents on the constitutional provisions concerning education are scarce and not altogether reliable.To this extent, Whyte readily admits that much of what he has to say in 'necessarily speculative' and that therefore other interpretations of the Constitution are also possible.

On the power of the State to prescribe a minimum standard of education, he comments that the only existing judicial authority on this matter – the *School Attendance Bill reference*, decided in 1943 – is now somewhat out-dated and therefore may not offer much assistance to contemporary policy makers.

Turning to the provision of primary education, the Supreme Court decision in *Crowley v. Ireland* emphasises that the State is not obliged to educate, but merely to provide an infrastructure for primary education. This distinction would appear to offer constitutional protection for the existing arrangements for the management of primary schools.

Finally, in teasing out some of the constitutional implications for State financing of denominational education, he identifies a tension within the Constitution between a policy of support for denominational education and a policy of neutrality towards the financing of religion generally. While the Constitution clearly allows the State to offer financial support to denominational education, the constitutional principle of non-endowment of religion may limit the extent of that support. Whyte attempts to identify acceptable interpretations of that principle of non-endowment and then applies these interpretations to the funding of Maynooth, teacher training colleges, chaplaincy and, finally, the integrated curriculum. He concludes that there may be constitutional doubts about these issues.

Each of the papers gave rise to valuable and wide-ranging discussion which would be impossible to summarise here. However, it should be noted, as a matter of record, that Gerry Whyte's paper provoked a lively exchange of views and the presentation of other interpretations of the non-endowment of religion clause in the Constitution. Some of these alternative interpretations are worth noting here. It was suggested that closer attention should be given to the origin and historical background of the verb 'to endow', having due regard to the 1922 Education Act and the disestablishment/disendowment of the Churches under English law as well as the current interpretation of the expression 'to endow' in the North of Ireland. Further, it was pointed out that the non-endowment clause could mean the non-endowment of any one particular religion to the exclusion of other religions. This particular interpretation, it was pointed out, also seemed closer to the Irish language version of the Constitution on this particular point. In addition, it was argued that the primary thrust of the Constitution is to support infrastructures favouring religion in general and denominational education in particular, and that therefore this should be the overriding context for interpreting the meaning of the non-endowment of religion and not vice versa. It was also observed that the meaning of endowment is really about the establishment of funds from which income could be derived to sustain something in perpetuity and that this is the primary intent of the clause relating to the non-endowment of religion.

OTHER ASPECTS OF THE DEBATE

The issues addressed in this collection of essays are clearly selective in scope. The volume deals deliberately only with some of the underlying religious, philosophical and legal aspects of education. Other aspects of the proposed reform of education in Ireland could have been addressed. Some of these should be mentioned here in passing with a view to enlarging the context in which the papers might be read and interpreted.

The first of these is about the importance of establishing some kind of consensus concerning educational priorities for the future. Because of the difficulty in reaching consensus, some have suggested a neutral point of departure in the present educational debate. It should be noted that legal or philosophical neutrality in education has its own agenda. It is hard to see how the assumptions which underly the notion of neutrality can do justice to the uniqueness, dignity and destiny of the individual. Further, if education in its most elementary sense is about drawing out the potential that is given in each person, then neutrality is hardly sustainable. In addition, if education is committed to serving the common good and promoting human values, then it is difficult to see how neutrality, including State neutrality, can be adopted as a point of departure or as a principle of interpretation.

The second of these relates to the role of the different Churches in education. All of the Christian Churches have played an important role in Irish education over the centuries, especially the Religious Orders of the Catholic Church. It is essential that the Churches be allowed to make their unique contribution to the national debate about education at primary, secondary and tertiary levels. They will make this contribution by keeping alive the saving memory and reality of Jesus Christ in the world of education through word and sacrament and service. In particular, the Churches will seek continually to retrieve the prophetic traditions of Judaism and Christianity by fostering a liberating *praxis* for justice, peace and reconciliation in our land, while resisting in hope the contemporary currents of consumerism and secularism in the name of the coming Reign of God. These activities will be promoted in and through the respective Religious Education programmes of the Churches in primary and secondary schools.

When it comes to third level education, we are faced with the extraordinary anomaly in Ireland that the Christian Churches have no theological place or educational presence in our universities due to the 1908 Universities Act. The State in Ireland makes no direct provision for the study of Theology or Religious Education in our publicly funded universities. This strange *lacuna* must be a matter of grave concern to all the Churches and the State. This particular absence of publicly funded Theology and/or Religious Education means in effect that there is very little interdisciplinary contact with serious religious questions and that a kind of spiritual silence or awkwardness surrounds the third level study of the Humanities, the sciences and the traditional professions. If Theology and Religious Education are not taken seriously as subjects of third level study, then this will have an effect on the way religion is viewed in public life. Is this a desirable state of affairs in terms of its consequences for the social, economic, political, cultural and commercial life of the country? How can the universities claim to be universities and yet exclude the study of the religious dimension of human experience and its revelation in Judaism, Christianity and other faiths? These are questions that the Minister for Education and the Higher Education Authority must begin to address. Ireland at present is one of the only countries in Europe in which Theology and Religious Education are not in receipt of public funding.

This strange situation seems to discriminate on religious grounds against students who might wish to study Theology and/or Religious Education at third level. Further, this anomalous situation means in effect that the parents of students attending privately run third level institutions, which do provide out of scarce resources for the study of Theology and Religious Education, are subject to a form of double taxation. These anomalies can hardly be deemed just or defensible in a country whose cultural heritage and historical traditions have been significantly influenced by Christianity.

A third issue concerns ecumenism within primary and secondary Religious Education. The ecumenical issue in Christian education must be faced by all the Christian Churches in Ireland. From a Catholic point of view, it must be acknowledged that the Second Vatican Council committed the Catholic Church formally and explicitly to the pursuit of Christian unity. The *Decree on Ecumenism* talks about the Catholic Church making the first approaches in ecumenical endeavours (a.4). To this extent, ecumenism must begin to assume a more visible profile in Catholic Religious Education programmes.

While there are some who wish to pursue what is often called multi-denominational education or inter-denominational education within the school system, this commendable ecumenical ideal may not be quite as easily attainable in practice as is assumed. Ecumenism is not about establishing the lowest common denominator among the Churches, nor is ecumenism about a *quid pro quo* among the Christian denominations, nor is ecumenism about paring down differences between the Churches. Rather, ecumenism is about recognising the need for reform from within an already established specific Christian tradition and identity. The recognition of this need for ecclesial reform and the desire for Christian unity is activated through the encounter among self-consciously committed Christians from different traditions. The experience of division and separation among different Christian denominations is one of the chief catalysts of real ecumenism. To this extent, well-intentioned calls for multi-denominational schooling or non-denominational religious education may require closer educational, ecumenical and theological scrutiny. What sets out to be ecumenical may unwittingly end up being counterproductive by giving rise to a bland awareness of Christianity and failing to communicate an active faith. Important lessons could be learned in this regard from experiments in other countries. If it is true that there is no such thing as non-denominational Christian theology, then it must be said that there is no such thing as non-denominational Christian Religious Education.

On the other hand, denominational schools do have a serious responsibility to engage in an ecumenical outreach to other denominational schools. Indeed, the denominational school that does not have ecumenical contact with other Christian denominations is neither true to its own Christian identity nor to the ecumenical movement. Consequently, denominational Religious Education programmes in schools need to have a more explicit ecumenical mandate and mission as part of their syllabi.

A fourth and final point which should be mentioned here concerns the image of religion in some discussions about education. There is a popular perception which sometimes presents religion as an isolated and separate aspect of life. Within this perspective, religion, more specifically Christianity, is understood as something purely private, separate, external and supernaturalistic. Where this understanding of Christianity has currency, then Christian faith is marginalised very quickly, becoming a mere appendix to life rather than an integral part of it, a piece of decoration added on here and there for cosmetic purposes. This not unpopular perception is inconsistent with the perspectives of Christian revelation and faith as well as tradition. The heart of Christianity is to be found in the mystery of the Incarnation, that unique historical event which brings together into a new unity God and the world, the human and the divine in the reality of Jesus Christ. The mere juxtaposition of the supernatural order to the natural order without any real relationship ends up denying the Incarnation. It is this kind of dualism that has given rise in this

13

century to a humanism without God and a theology without humanism. Likewise, Christian faith, founded on the Incarnation, does have social and public implications. It is a contradiction in terms to claim Christian identity and at the same time to live life alone and privately. Individual Christian faith is social and communitarian.

Dualistic separations of the sacred and the secular, of nature and grace, and of the personal and the social have been stubbornly refused down through the centuries by the teachings of different Christian Churches in their Councils and Synods. The temptation to separate Christian faith and culture must be equally refused today in discussions about the relationship between religion and education. The strength of the Christian faith is its capacity to unify diversity and integrate opposites without confusing them. In this sense, religion, more specifically Christian faith, permeates the whole of life transforming the world into a creation, the secular into the sacramental, the ordinary into the mystical.

For these reasons, it would be a step backwards in Ireland if we were to set out on a path separating religion and education. The right and necessary distinction between Church and State, properly understood, does not demand a separation between religion and education. Instead, as the papers by John Hull, Kevin Williams and Eoin Cassidy clearly show, religion has an important critique to offer education, and education in its turn challenges religion to address the important issues of the day.

Dermot A. Lane

I. Religion and Education in a pluralist society

John M. Hull

Thank you very much for your warm welcome. It is an honour to be present at the 25th Anniversary of this distinguished Institution which I have visited before under happier circumstances than the one I find myself in tonight, but I am sure I will feel much happier about it tomorrow!

Religious education is undergoing something of a resurgence. In many of the countries of Eastern Europe, where religious education only two or three years ago was actually forbidden, its place occupied by compulsory materialistic and atheistic education, it has become a compulsory subject. *The British Journal of Religious Education* in January 1992 will be publishing an article on the resurgence of religious education in Russia.[1] We can also think of the revival of religious education in Germany, stimulated by the unification and by the presence of the Turkish community.[2] I must also refer to the 1988 Educational Reform Act (England & Wales) which may be regarded as a kind of resurgence of religious education. What kind of resurgence is a matter of debate, but that it has been accompanied by a considerable increase of public, political and professional interest in what religious education should be doing is undoubtedly the case.[3] We have, for example, in 1988 the change in status of the Standing Advisory Councils for Religious Education (SACRE) which every local education authority in England and Wales is now required to establish. [4]

What I have to share with you this evening falls under four headings. First, religious education as the study of religion, second, religious education as the critique of religion, third, religious education as a gift to human development, and finally, religious education as Christian mission.

1. RELIGIOUS EDUCATION AS THE STUDY OF RELIGION

When we ask what religious education is, the most obvious answer is that religious education is the study of religion. Beneath that apparently simple answer lie a number of perplexities. What is religion and how is it to be studied? By whom is it to be studied and who is to control the study of it? The study of religion can itself be considered from a number of different points of view, forming a series of philosophical and educational problems. My colleague in the University of Birmingham, Michael Grimmit, has distinguished between learning religion, learning about religion, and learning from religion.[5] Religious education as learning religion would be the transmissional view of religious education, religious education as that which transmits religious culture, belief and values, religious education as responsible for the perpetuation, the survival, the handing on of the tradition. Here one learns religion. We can also think of religious education as learning about religion, that view of the study of religion which looks upon it in a purely objective and descriptive manner where one no longer learns religion in the sense of absorbing it or receiving it but in the sense of knowing facts about it. This way of teaching religion in the English tradition, goes back to the early 19th century. It is out of that historical critical approach to the Bible that religious education slowly evolved in the course of the twentieth century.[6] We may regard this approach, and some of the more factually objective forms of teaching religion today, as being various examples of teaching about religion.

If we consider Michael Grimmitt's third distinction – learning not about religion but from religion – we have an interesting perspective, a more educational perspective, one which asks what is the educational advantage to be gained by the study of religion. How can one learn from religion? What is there to learn from religion? What is it that boys and girls and men and women have today to learn from religion which is valuable for their lives? In what way can the study of religion illuminate the problems of human living? I will return to this under my third heading, Religious Education as a gift to human development.

When we start to talk about religious education in this way in a pluralist context, we realise that the study of religion cannot be confined to the study of one religion. Nearly everyone recognises this today. There has been much discussion in England and Wales about the precise balance between the teaching of Christianity and other religions.[7] In 1988 there was a strong movement (which was successful) to name Christianity in the Act as a compulsory religion. The final text of the 1988 Act is an ambiguous compromise. Section 8 (3) says that any new agreed syllabus shall

> reflect the fact that the principal religious traditions of Great Britain are in the main Christian whilst taking account of the teaching and practices of the other principal religions represented in Great Britain.

That sentence is carefully balanced. The agreed syllabuses shall reflect the fact that the principal religious traditions of Great Britain are in the main Christian; this is balanced by the second part of the sentence; whilst taking account of the teaching and practices of the other principal religions. Interpretation of these words has ranged from those who have emphasised the first part, that agreed syllabuses must reflect Christianity, (therefore they must be *based* on Christianity, they must be *Christian* agreed syllabuses, Christianity must *predominate*) to those who have emphasised that what is significant is that world religions, the teaching of religious education through the study of the religions of the world, is now formally established by law. No agreed syllabus can be legal if it fails to take account of the teaching and practices of the principal religions represented in the country.

The Government, in seeking to define the content of religious education, has made a rod for its own back. The definition is supported by a complaints procedure which has been used by groups of parents who are dissatisfied with the religious teaching being received in their schools. The Government has been obliged to rule on these various complaints. This has led to a closer and closer definition of the clause I quoted a moment ago. This is to be found in the two letters circulated from the Department of Education and Science in March and in August of 1991. The March 18th letter contains the significant expression that no agreed syllabus can be legal if any principal religion represented in Great Britain is omit-

17

ted. But what is a principal religion? What has to happen in order for it to be represented in Great Britain? The inexorable logic of further legal complaints may compel the Government to draw up a list of principal religions, and to define statistically what representation signifies. We will then be back in the days of the Roman Empire with a list of civil religions acceptable to the state. Protesting groups will besiege Whitehall demanding to receive principal religion status. Any such content-rich definition is likely to lead to embarrassments of this sort.

When the transmission model of religious education is functional the question of control is fairly straightforward. The religion that is being transmitted controls the process of transmission. When however you are dealing with a pluralistic situation, where the study of religion embraces several faiths, there is a problem of who is to control. Shall the parents, the profession, or the Government control the curriculum? Shall the churches control? When religion as the object of study is controlled by the churches as the sponsors of study, the audit of quality will remain a problem. It is contrary to the principles of quality control that the sponsors of study should control their own teaching, that the objects of study should be in the control of those in whose interest it is that their own faith should be transmitted. That would represent a kind of control too narrow for the various value systems and pressure groups which constitute our modern, democratic society. We must therefore find forms of accountability where the objects of study although not excluded, do not have total power over the way in which they are studied. This question of the balance between the proper authority to be exercised by religions as the objects of study and the actual teaching of children in the schools is another question which is exercising many of the SACRE's in England. Various solutions are appearing.

In some areas an agreement has been reached between the profession and the religions, in which the religions will produce lists of what their principal teachings are so that the agreed syllabus can take account of them. The teachers are to mediate that content to their children in the form of a curriculum. The religions are to say what it is about them which is to be studied, but it is the teachers who are to say how, in what context, by what methods, in what sequences the material itself shall be presented to the children. That is quite an interesting way of arranging the respective roles of the religions and the teachers. This is a new form of the ancient tension between the priest and the teacher, a relationship which has an interesting shape in pluralism.

The solution to these problems lies in some properly constituted, consultative mechanism representing the various interested groups, a public arena set up by law where parents, teachers and religious groups, can properly negotiate what is to be taught. Without some such placing of control on a community basis, I do not see how religious education can ever move from the parochial setting of the transmission model into the wider sphere of the curriculum which is demanded by the cultural and social problems of today. For the Churches, the question is painful: whether to exercise control within a narrow and increasingly irrelevant sphere or to abandon control, i.e. to share power with other interested parties, thus establishing a spiritual presence in the heart of the secular curriculum. I shall return to this theme in the final part of this paper.

2. RELIGIOUS EDUCATION AS CRITIQUE OF RELIGION

The problem with religious education as the study of religion lies in the ambiguity of the phenomenon. Religion is a highly ambiguous matter.[8]

At this point we have to ask ourselves about distinctions between studying religion and studying mathematics or geography. Religion occupies a unique place in the ideology of a culture. Although mathematics and geography are far from free of ideological traces, religious matters serve ideological functions in a striking and central way. This is highlighted by the Marxian analysis of religion, which will become increasingly important now that the study of Marx has been freed from the political inhibition caused by the former communist regimes of the East. In the thought of Marx religion forms part of the super structure of society. This role is played not by mathematics, nor by geography, but by religion. In

19

industrial societies religion forms part of the over-arching framework of ideas, of culture, of presuppositions which serve as the mirror image of the industrial and economic base of that society. In medieval society the king is in his palace and the beggar is at his gate. This is the way God decreed it and so the earthly society mirrors the heavenly one. Similar but more complicated forms of superstructural religion abound in western culture today. In many of its modern forms religion is functioning as the mirror image of late industrial society. What are the implications for the way religious education is taught? Is it possible for a religious education which is itself a product and an expression of that super structure to mount a critique of itself?

We have to find some point of reference from which the study of the ambiguity of religion can be mounted. This moves religious education into the social sciences. In speaking of religious education as the study of religion, the social science basis was already obvious. Religion is to be studied by means of a number of disciplines including anthropology, history, psychology and others. When religious education is regarded as the study of religion, theology is already in the market place with other disciplines. When one turns to religious education as the critique of religion one moves from the normal social sciences into a more critical view of the nature of the social sciences themselves.

Jurgen Habermas has distinguished three types of subject, three principal disciplines which make up the modern universe of knowledge.[9] First there are the disciplines concerned with measurement and description such as physics, botany and biology, then those which are mainly concerned with interpretation such as history and psychology, and thirdly those which are concerned with human emancipation. He distinguishes thus between the descriptive disciplines, the interpretative disciplines, and the emancipatory disciplines. Amongst the latter he places Marxist economics and Freudian psycho-analysis. We can define religious education as one of the emancipatory disciplines within the critical social sciences, one whose goal is human freedom.

We can now conceive of religious education as performing tasks which go far beyond its role as comprising the study of religion. The task of religious education is to expose religion to itself, to reveal the ambiguity of religion in ways which liberate adults and children from the oppressive aspects of religion, and at the same time to open up the treasures of religion, its liberating and life affirming aspects to human beings.

We may now compare religious education with deep sources of human energy, inspiration and deception like those lying within our sexuality. Religion has a power and an ambiguity both to transform and to deceive, both to build up and to destroy, similar to that of our human sexuality. Both are fundamental in energising basic human nature, both are characterised by elements of regression, of infantile fixations, both have a tendency to become fetishised, i.e. to take symbolic parts in place of wholes. They are the source of the most tragic wastefulness and also the source of our most sublime and creative human relationships. If religion is to be looked at in that way, then religious education like sexual education must adopt a critical stance. It cannot take its phenomena for granted but must adopt a critical approach towards them. The sex educationalists are dealing with something which is presented to them already. Young people bring sex into the classroom with them. So it is with religion. Young people come into the classroom with their infantile gods under their arms[10] and with the whole cultural super structure of the ideological function carried out by religion already embedded.

Ideology is that within which our identity is embedded. The ideology consists in the surrounding and unconsciously accepted framework of values, beliefs and assumptions which are so much the groundwork of our identity that we do not even notice them. Paul Ricoeur has remarked that we cannot notice our ideologies because they are not in front of our eyes; they are behind our backs. We cannot argue for them because they are the ground upon which we argue.[11] Ideology is also the reification or the projection into a belief structure of the features of our socio-political and economic life.

Finally, ideology enables groups to articulate their identities. Such ideologies enable groups to achieve historical significance. The ideology gives direction to the project of the group in the world. By the same token, ideologies have a tendency to tribalise the groups which adhere to them. It is characteristic of modern Europe that the resurgence of religion is accompanied by a revival of tribalised nationalism. Yugoslavia offers an instructive case of this. After decades of communist rule when religious distinctions were suppressed, people voted along religious and tribalistic lines at the first opportunity. Orthodox Christians voted for Orthodox politicians, Catholics voted for Catholics, Muslims voted for Muslims, and so on. The same thing is taking place in many of the Republics of the former Soviet Union.

These events illustrate the extraordinary power of religious traditions to confer identity upon groups which then become tribalised in that identity. By tribalisation I mean the way in which religions confer identity through exclusion. I am Christian precisely because I am not Muslim; I am Protestant precisely because I am not Catholic; I am a Christian precisely because I am not Asian. At this point the connection between religious identity and racism becomes rather obvious.

In these forms of exclusive identity-creation, awareness of identity becomes inflamed in times of conflict. The result is a form of delirious perception. The other, the alien, the one against whom I assert my own identity by negation and exclusion becomes a stereotype.

Now the characteristic mechanisms of ideology come into play. No longer for example does history create the Jew (which is the truth) but we have its ideological inversion, the Jew now becomes the one who creates history. Thus emerges the typology of the Jewish conspiracy to create modern Europe, and the reifications of Judaism as the alter-ego of the Arian race, and the delirious perception which conferred power and charisma upon Jews, which finally led to Auschwitz.

These forms of delirious perception lie beneath the surface of our own society. Religious education must grapple with the relationship between identity, ideology, tribalisation and nationalism in a time of multinational mixing. Above all, it must tackle the delirious perception which leads to this stereotypical view of the other, another from whom one must separate; one must dread the contamination of contact with such aliens. Finally one must engage in conflict in order to extinguish the opponent in the interests of one's own identity.

When we examine the Decade of Evangelism currently under way in England we find similar problems of tribalism, nationalism and delirious perception. This then, is the sort of thing I mean when I talk about religious education as offering a critique of religion. It can be done with young children as well as with adults. These concepts can be interpreted pedagogically for very young children as for older ones. A teacher in a nursery school was telling me recently that when she sought to gather examples of nursery rhymes from her children there was not a child in her class who knew any. All they could do was sing television jingles. These children already emptied of traditional culture are being filled by commercial jingles, being set up to enter the consumer culture. If we consider the way in which religion and the market co-operate at Christmas time to turn children into receptacles for all manner of things, we find in a simple way much of what I have been talking about. Religious education is capable of tackling these problems in a manner appropriate to children of every age and level of ability. This critique of religion is also an essential responsibility of adult education within the churches. This however implies that not all religion is false, not all is super structural, that not all religion is a mere mirror imaging of a tribalistic identity. If there is a false religion there is a true. This brings us to our third section.

3. RELIGIOUS EDUCATION AS A GIFT TO HUMAN DEVELOPMENT

One of the weaknesses of religious education considered simply as the study of religion lies in the inability of religious studies under the domination of uncritical social sciences to distinguish between true religion and false. Indeed the phenomenological method which brackets out such evaluation would say that such distinctions were not only irrelevant but scientifically illegitimate. This is however false to the ideological nature of religion. In the epistle of James (1:27) we read that 'pure and undefiled religion' is to 'visit orphans and widows in their affliction.' If there is a pure religion there is an impure religion, and an approach to religious education which is unable to make the distinction between the pure and the impure cannot get beyond the study of religion. It cannot understand religious education as a critique of religion because the very pre-suppositions of critique are not granted as being possible by a view of the study of religion which refuses to distinguish pure from impure religion. If false religion leads to delirious perception and tribalisation, true religion lends genuine dignity, autonomy and communion to human beings. In that sense religious education is a gift to human development.

In Birmingham we have created what we think is a new approach to the teaching of religion to young children.[12] We have developed ways to present the beauty and holiness of religion to young children directly, almost without preliminaries. Our technique is to confront children immediately with the direct representations of religion in its beauty and holiness. Through a variety of teaching techniques we invite children to identify themselves with these holy objects and realities, but then to retreat and to distance themselves. We have created a series of techniques which we call 'entering devices' which enable children to identify with the materials, and 'distancing devices' which protect them from inappropriate intimacy. We are discovering that through this teaching technique it is possible for religious education to give gifts to children. This is an empirical claim and we hope to start a three-year project in which we shall seek to assess it. We hope to discover whether this kind of religious education has equipped the imaginations of children in such a way as to deepen their vocabulary, to give them greater curiosity, to deepen their empathy, to strengthen their faith in the case of those children who have faith, to heighten their sense of dignity and independence in the case of children who do not come from religious families, and thus to offer gifts to the general education and human development of children.

Not all the gifts of religion need themselves be religious. Thoth, the god of wisdom in Ancient Egypt, gave his people not only religion but writing, medicine, culture, literature and poetry. All these gifts came from the gods. Similarly not all the gifts of religious education need be religious. Religious education can give secular gifts to human development. These are available not only to those who believe in religion, but to those who study it. It would be curious if religious education did not offer religious gifts. Accordingly the distinction between religious nurture and religious education which was so important ten or fifteen years ago is less significant today. While we should carefully distinguish those children who are to study religion from those children who are also to be nurtured in religion, both functions of religious education are possible and legitimate. If, however, religious education succeeds in deepening identity and in opening each to the other, it will occupy a unique position in the spirituality and morality of the curriculum.

4. RELIGIOUS EDUCATION AS CHRISTIAN MISSION

In the last paragraph of his famous sermon 'The Yoke of Religion' written more than forty years ago, Paul Tillich said this about the teaching of Christianity.

> It would not be worthwhile to teach Christianity, if it were for the sake of Christianity. And believe me, you who are estranged from Christianity, it is not our purpose to make you religious and Christian when we interpret the call of Jesus for our time. We call Jesus the Christ not because He brought a new religion, but because He is the end of religion, above religion and irreligion, above Christianity and non-Christianity. We spread His call because it is the call to every man in every period to receive the New Being ... [13]

It is not worthwhile teaching Christianity if it is taught merely as Christianity. What does this mean? We have to distinguish between a Christian religious education which seeks to propagate itself and a Christian religious education which seeks to serve humanity. Need these two things be different? They need not be, but such is the ambiguity of religion that they may be different. We have seen already how certain kinds of Christian religious education far from serving humanity serve only to tribalise humanity by building up delirious perception.Christian identity is itself ambiguous. This can be illustrated by contrasting two approaches towards a theology of evangelism.

First there is a theology of evangelism which is a supplanting approach, i.e. the view that evangelism consists in seeking to replace Muslim beliefs in my Muslim friend by Christian beliefs. Faith in Islam would be supplanted. Its place will be taken by Christian belief so at the end of the day there will no longer be any Muslims, or Sikhs left in the world. They will all have become Christians. It is regrettable that many Christians adopt this view because it feeds tribal identities. It seeks to reinforce tribal identities by glorying in the cessation of other identities. Authentic Christian mission must scrutinize this view and religious education must carefully distance itself from it.

The second theology of evangelism draws upon the mission of Jesus, the work of the Galilean Christ as recorded in the synoptic gospels. In the life and teaching of Jesus of Nazareth there is little or no trace of a supplanting view of evangelism. There is little evidence that Jesus was interested in getting other people to share his religious views. He had plenty of opportunities to do so. In the fourth chapter of John's Gospel the Samaritan woman tried to draw Jesus into a dispute between religions with the question 'our fathers worshipped on this mountain, and you say that in Jerusalem is the place where we ought to worship'. Would Jesus seek to supplant Samaritan faith with genuine Jewish faith? No. Jesus was completely indifferent to the question. 'Neither on this mountain nor in Jerusalem will you worship the Father...true worshippers will worship the Father in spirit and truth.' (Jn 4:21, 23). Indeed he spoke somewhat critically of those who cross sea and land to make one proselyte, to gain one convert. (Matt 23:15). What then was the mission of Jesus? In Luke, Chapters 9 and 10, we find that it was not a mission which sought to transplant beliefs from one position to another but one which sought to heal the sick and to announce the coming of the Kingdom of God. (Luke 9:1; 10:9). When religious education is described as a min-

istry of healing and emancipation, a criticism is sometimes lev-
elled against it. Christianity it is said, is being *used*. It has now
become instrumental and is used by education for purposes other
than those intrinsic to Christianity itself.

At this point a fundamental question about the nature of the
Christian faith itself arises. Is it the mission of Christianity today
to propagate itself or to serve humanity? If Christianity is to be
inspired by Jesus Christ the answer is clear. Christianity did not
emerge as a religion amongst the religions of the world in opposition to them. It emerged as a vision of a new humanity, in which
Greek and Jew, circumcised and the uncircumcised (distinctions
between religions), male and female, slaves and free, would all be
one, (Gal 3:28; Col 3:11), the Christ person in whom all these distinctions were overcome and made into one glorious mishmash.
(2 Cor 5:17). Separation, however, is very important to many religious people and the distinctions between the religious traditions
are held to be extremely significant. That does not seem to me to
be the view of the New Testament or of Jesus. Let us take the situation where Peter had the vision of the great sheet lowered down
from heaven (Acts 10:11). In the sheet were all sorts of animals
representing various taboos which Peter had been faithfully
taught to observe, holy and sacred things about his faith, things
which should have been carefully separate and distinct from one
another, all jumbled up together in a glorious mishmash. A voice
from heaven said 'Rise, Peter, kill and eat.' Peter said 'No, Lord,
because I have never eaten anything which is common or unclean.' He did not want to be contaminated by such a failure to
distinguish. The answer came 'What God has cleaned you must
not call unclean.'

Let us take one final example of an instrumental view of Christian
faith. On the Sabbath day Jesus is watched in the synagogue by
the Pharisees and the Scribes to see what he will do about a man
with a withered hand who has come into the synagogue to seek
healing. Jesus said to the man 'Come and stand here.' They all
watched to see what he would do. Looking around upon them
Jesus said 'I ask you, is it lawful on the sabbath to do good or to do
harm, to save life or to destroy it?' When they made no reply he

27

said to the man 'Stretch out your hand,' and it was made whole. (Luke 6:6-11). Here we see a prophet who was unwilling to accept the distinctions, the legitimate and necessary structures of self-perpetuation which had been transmitted to him by his own spiritual tradition. This reminds us of the saying 'People were not made for the Sabbath but the Sabbath for people.' (Mark 2:27). If that was said by Jesus of the Sabbath, the most central and sacred institution of his own tradition, should we not as inheritors of the Spirit of Jesus say it also of our own faith? People were not made for Christianity but Christianity for people. We must regard the whole of the Christian tradition as being used by God in a divine mission which is greater than Christianity, of which Christianity is the servant, and which points to the Kingdom of God. My understanding of religious education can be summed up in the expression 'out of pain into pain'. Religious education is to enable young people and adults to be delivered from their own personal pain and to shoulder the pain of the world. But how can the pure and the impure in religion be distinguished? The answer is a fairly simple one. Every religious image, doctrine or tradition which opens people up to human pain is a pure religion. Every religion which closes people off from human pain is an impure religion.

The task of religious education then is to enable young people, under the stimulus of the religious and Christian imagery, and in the context of the spiritual traditions of all humanity, to mature out of their own pain and thus to embrace the pain of all humanity. In this way the mission of Christianity may be fulfilled by pointing us all towards the Kingdom of God.

The Mission of Religious Education in England and Ireland. Although the different approaches to religious education which we have been considering may be thought of as universal types, international comparisons cannot leap from the concrete characteristics of particular traditions to conclusions about policy merely by means of these abstract types. From the point of view of scholarship and the exchange of ideas, religious education is no doubt part of the global village, but at the same time, the legal framework within which it operates from one nation state to another is part of the historical legacy of each country. Every actual religious education

28

has been shaped by the history of religions between religions, between religion and state, as well as religion and religion. Even the expression 'religious education' means different things in different countries.

Religious education in England and Ireland has been influenced by the different character which pluralism has taken. English Christianity became pluralistic in the 16th century with the emergence of distinctions between Catholicism and Protestanism, and within Protestanism distinctions between Presbyterianism, Congregationalism and others. The Quakers appeared in the 17th century, Methodists in the 18th, while Catholic emancipation put Roman Catholicism back into the denominational marketplace in the early 19th century. With the coming of the ecumenical movement in the 20th century, the Agreed Syllabus emerged as the management structure for curriculum decision-making in a pluralist society. Between 1920 and 1970, however, the emphasis was upon agreement rather than upon plurality. The Agreed Syllabus was a device for enabling a single (although reduced) Christian world view to be presented in spite of pluralism.

From the late 1960's or early 1970's a change came over English religious education which has to be interpreted sociologically as well as educationally. Plurality was no longer disguised but studied. It was no longer a problem but an educational opportunity. Over a period of about 20 years, a new consensus was formed. This was inspired mainly by liberalism, and by the scholarly study of religion using phenomenology as its technique. The nurturing of faith was seen as the task of the religious community or Church while the State religious curriculum was dedicated to increasing an understanding of religion in a pluralist context.

This pluralist context was no longer confined to the Christian traditions but embraced the major religions of the world. This widening of the horizons was not only linked to the increased ethnic diversity of the English population, especially in the industrial cities, but to an increasing awareness of the dangers of a Euro-centred approach. Moreover, religious radicalism was no longer taking a merely secularist and existentialist form as it had been during the 1960's, but was increasingly influenced by justice and peace issues, informed by a more sophisticated social and historical understanding of the role of religion. Religious education was now not only seen as making a contribution to the search for a faith to live by on the part of the individual student, but as having a role to play in the conscientisation of the school community, the entire curriculum, religious groups and family life. Religious education became increasingly aware of the ambiguity of its position towards racism, the oppression of women and the perpetuation of the structures of economic injustice.

These trends, both in religion and in religious education, did not go unchallenged, nor was the conflict confined to religion. The 1988 Education Reform Act may be regarded as the triumph of conservatism. An attempt was made to restore the instructional model based on Christianity. The 'integrity' of each religious tradition was not seen as central to religious education, and the ideal pattern would be a separate faith instruction, from Christian teachers to Christian children, with similar rights extended to children from other faiths. This is not the place to examine these trends in detail, but enough has been said to see some striking contrasts and similarities with the situation in Ireland.

In the Republic of Ireland, pluralism has been relatively slight. An attempt was made to solve significant differences between Catholic and Protestant by territorial demarcation, leaving the northern counties as the cockpit of conflict. In the south, Christian instruction conceived mainly in doctrinal terms under Church patronage but informed by a generally tolerant spirit of openness and enquiry occupied the field, whilst in the north two systems of instruction faced each other, each bound intimately into struggles about identity and culture.

I will not make any attempt to comment on the painful situation in Northern Ireland. As for the Republic, the first question is the relationship between religious society and secular society, between religious tradition and the character of the State. If this can be solved in a manner so as to make possible the participation of religious education in the curriculum as a whole, in some way that is professionally, educationally and culturally respectable, the next issue will undoubtedly be pluralism. Monolithic instructional traditions when penetrated by the needs of a secular society cannot resist the widening horizons of world religions. If the English experience is anything to go by, and we have seen how profoundly different it is, this stage of religious pluralism will bring about a conservative reaction which will lead to the radicalisation of the mission of religious education.

With some caution, we may discern the outline of three consecutive stages in the development of religious education in modern national states. Monoreligious traditional instruction gives way to multi-cultural education for understanding. This in turn becomes dialectical through controversy, leading to a heightened awareness of the ambiguity of religion and a reformation of the goals of religious education in the direction of the Kingdom of God, of the ideals of international peace and justice.

This three-stage theory is made more complex when we place Ireland and England within the context of the European community, and of the wider geographical and economic space of Europe as a whole. The question of religious education within Europe turns into the question of the relationship between Europe and the rest of the world. Is religious education about to enter a new period of Christian conservatism, when European culture and Christian tradition will be increasingly identified with each other, to their mutual satisfaction? Or are we entering a period of repentance, when the relationship between Christian faith and European culture will be seen in dialectical terms, so that Christian faith urges European religious education away from the gods of the European dream toward the God of all people?

For modern European religious education, the man from Macedonia, who first appeared in a vision to Saint Paul calling Christianity from Asia into Europe, is now experienced in reverse. Instead of the man from Macedonia, modern religious education is haunted

31

by the child from the streets and the sewers of Bogota. My child is lost in the sewers of Bogota, Colombia, and I must go and find him. A religious education which thus strives to bring young people and adults out of pain and into pain will be an educational enterprise worthy of Christian discipleship.

Notes:

1   Mark Halstead, 'Recent Developments in Religious Education in Russia,' *British Journal of Religious Education*, Vol. 15, No. 2, Spring 1992, pp. 99-106.

2   A number of papers delivered at the Fourth Nuremberg Conference on Religious Education (September 1991) will shortly appear in the *BJRE*.

3   For a broad educational interpretation of the religious requirements of the Act, see my booklet *The Act Unpacked, the Meaning of the 1988 ERA for Religious Education*, Derby: CEM, 1989.

4   Monica J. Taylor, *SACREs: Their Formation, Composition, Operation and Role on RE and Worship, A Report of Research Sponsored by the National Curriculum Council in 1990*. National Foundation for Educational Research, 1991.

5   Michael H. Grimmitt, 'When is "Commitment" a Problem in RE?' in *British Journal of Educational Studies*, 29, No.1, 1981, pp. 42-53.

6   I have discussed learning the Bible, learning about the Bible, and learning from the Bible in the last part of my lecture *The Bible in the Secular Classroom: An Approach Through the Experience of Loss*, Durham: North of England Institute of Christian Education, 1986.

7   John M. Hull, 'Agreed Syllabuses and the Law', *Resource* (PCfRE), Vol. 14, No.2, September 1991, pp. 1-3, and 'Should the Agreed Syllabuses be Mainly Christian?' *BJRE*, Vol. 14, No. 1, Autumn 1991, pp. 1-3.

8   The ambiguity of religion is the main theme of my Inaugural Lecture *Religion, Education and Madness – a Modern Trinity*, School of Education, University of Birmingham, 1991.

9   Jurgen Habermas, *Knowledge and Human Interests*, Boston: Beacon Press, 1971.

10   'No child arrives at the house of God without his birth god under his arm', Ana Marie Rizuto, *The Birth of the Living God: a Psychoanalytic Study*, Chicago and London: Chicago University Press, 1979, p. 8.

11   Paul Ricoeur, 'Science and Ideology', *Hermeneutics and the Human Sciences*, Cambridge: University Press, 1981, pp.222ff.

12   Michael H. Grimmitt, Julie Grove, John M. Hull and Louise Spencer, *A Gift to the Child, Religious Education in the Primary School*, London: Simon and Schuster, 1991.

13   Paul Tillich, *The Shaking of the Foundations*, London: SCM Press, 1949, p. 102.

II. Usefulness and Liberal Learning

Kevin Williams

I can imagine that many people must be asking themselves what could be the possible relationship between the subject of this essay and the proposed Education Act. The answer is quite simple. One of the fears of educators is that the spirit of the Act will endorse the current tendency to promote a fashionable and superficial notion of usefulness as an educational aim.[1] In an excellent article responding to this tendency, the philosopher, Mary Midgley, draws attention to an 'important ambiguity' in the notion of usefulness in educational discourse and calls for 'much sharper criticism' of the way the term is employed.[2] By raising questions about the plausibility of usefulness as an educational aim, this essay attempts to identify the direction such a criticism might take. The article also offers a characterisation and defence of the notion of liberal learning and concludes with a consideration of the implications of its arguments for curriculum design.

1. ON USEFULNESS

As is common among philosophers I should like to start by making some distinctions. Useful can be employed in several different senses. In one sense it can mean *the point or the value* of something as when we respond to a question regarding the use of studying Latin or music. In another sense (what it is proposed to call the *instrumental sense*) we talk of using something as a *means* to something else in the manner in which a person might learn Irish in order to get a job in the Civil Service or someone might work in a restaurant in order to earn the money to study Latin at university, or study Latin at university with a view to getting a job as a graduate manager with a restaurant chain. The term is also used as a synonym for *practical* and as a contrast with the *theoretical*. Here we might make a further two distinctions between the *manual/intellectual* and the *applicable/academic*. Learning to cook is useful in

34

the sense of being *practical/manual*, while studying the chemistry of the ingredients, being intellectual activity, is not useful in this sense. However, study of the chemistry of common cooking ingredients yields potentially *applicable* knowledge and so can be said to be useful, whereas studying medieval art is not useful in the sense of being *applicable* to practical tasks. Usually when people speak of usefulness with regard to the school curriculum, they mean *directly useful in a vocational sense*, in the manner in which keyboard skills or accounting skills, for example, might be said to be useful. Although the employment envisaged is usually conceived in terms of the production of wealth, it does not have to be conceived in these terms. For example, a student may be encouraged to study music in school solely with a view to getting the non-wealth producing job of a musician. For the purposes of this paper, however, usefulness is meant to be understood in the sense of direct usefulness for productive employment or what might be called vocationalism. Let us turn therefore to a consideration of the plausibility of vocationalism as an educational aim.

Usefulness and productive employment. In expressing fears about the possible thrust of the Education Act with regard to curricular policy, we must not be led to exaggerate the demand for vocationalism in education, particularly at second level. It is important not to construct and demolish philosophical straw men through the assertion of well-meaning but ill informed platitudes. No reputable writer on education advocates economic usefulness as the sole aim of schooling and it is too easy to 'fire petulant salvoes from the good ship "Rational-liberalism" against the evil batteries of "Utilitarian-materialism".'[3] Moreover, what may be found counter-intuitive, is that a recent survey of industrialists in this country reveals a considerable level of satisfaction with the way schools are meeting the needs of industry.[4] And what may also be found surprising is that a recent large scale survey indicates that skill shortages have been almost entirely eliminated from the labour market in Ireland.[5] Demands to promote a closer articulation between the school curriculum and the economy reflect popular and governmental assumptions rather than a fully worked out position. These assumptions are often given expression in the standard criticism of the educational system for not being practical

enough.[6] The popular view is reflected, for example, in the arguments used to promote, on grounds of their utility, the teaching of
foreign languages languages in schools.[7] It is given dramatic
expression in the increased subscription to what are perceived as
economically relevant subjects at second level and in the frantic
demand for business courses at third level.[8] The irony here is of
course that business studies, unlike science and technology, are
concerned with the management, rather than with the production, of wealth. But, despite this trend, the curriculum in Irish
schools remains overwhelmingly liberal in character. [9]

The burden of the argument of this section of the paper is that a
vibrant productive economy does not require a direct relationship
between the school curriculum and the world of work. The
attempt to promote economic productivity directly through the
curriculum is misguided because employment opportunities are
related to the state of the economy rather than to the character of
the educational system. Where there are jobs, the employment
market adapts to the educated talent which is available in any
society. Some reflection on the recent history of Italy and Japan is
instructive here. Both of these countries have enjoyed great economic success since the Second World War but, as John Vaizey
points out, in both cases 'the education system was vestigial in
terms of providing people with skills, and ... the relationship
between the employment system and the education system was
singularly unarticulated.'[10] The experience of these countries
demonstrates the fallacy of the view of education as the means
whereby 'human capital' becomes developed. In any case, if possession of skills of putative vocational utility became more wide-
spread, this would simply intensify competition for a relatively
fixed number of jobs. Attention should also be drawn to one sinis-
ter danger of attributing unemployment to lack of educational
qualifications; this is the danger that unemployment comes to be
attributed to lack of qualifications on the part of individuals rather than to structural inequalities in society. As research indicates,
employment opportunities are related to socio-political considerations rather than to technical qualifications. In other words, position and influence within the socio-economic hierarchy are more
important in securing employment than one's qualifications. [11]

Let us turn next to a consideration of the relationship between education and employment by examining some statistics on actual employment patterns. For example, 57 per cent of the Labour force works in the services sector, 28 per cent in industry and 15 per cent in agriculture. Apart from teachers, nurses, members of the Garda Síochána and of the defence forces, many of those who work in the services sector are employed as routine clerical workers.[12] Analysis of statistics on employment patterns within the electrical and mechanical, electronic, chemical and allied products industries, reveals that half the employees in these industries are unskilled and only between 18 and 25 per cent could be described as technologically skilled.[13] Indeed, the *Labour Force Survey 1989* reveals that only 15.8 per cent of the entire labour force in Ireland could be classified as technical or professional. These statistics suggest that for the performance of most jobs people do not need to learn very much of direct vocational relevance – and certainly not in school. It can therefore be plausibly argued that the main contribution of education to economic productivity goes little beyond the provision of mass literacy. Moreover, the empirical research on the relationship between education and economic productivity provides scant evidence to support the claim that higher levels of education among employees lead to greater productivity.[14] Of course, there is also the argument that the real vocational purpose of the education system is to act as a selection mechanism for prestigious and well paid employment and to promote the qualities of compliant docility required by industry. Although there is some truth in the former claim and maybe even some also in the latter, lack of space prevents me pursuing these issues any further here.

It is hardly surprising therefore that research indicates that employers simply do not put a high value on vocationally 'relevant' skills in the recuitment of both scholl leavers and graduates. The Irish research referred to previously, which is borne out by research internationally, confirms the low value placed by employers on studies of direct vocational relevance. For example, only 18 and 25 per cent of employers surveyed rated familiarity with computer systems and keyboard skills as very important.[15]

A wry illustration of this general point is provided by the claim of influential industrialist, Sir Douglas Hague, that for those wishing to work in information and management, the study of philosophy provides more appropriate preparation than the study of information and communication technology and even of computer science.[16] This leads to the question of what it is that employers actually want from potential employees.

What employers do in fact value in potential employees is a general education, together with the skills of accurate and effective communication, including the skills of literacy and numeracy and, above all, appropriate personal qualities. This is clear if we examine the order of very important ratings in the recent survey of employers. Oral communications were rated very important by 70 per cent of the respondents, written communications by 58 per cent, numeracy by 48 per cent, enterprise/initiative by 46 per cent, problem solving by 39 per cent, foreign language skills by 26 per cent, creativity by 22 per cent, computer familiarity by 18 per cent, keyboard skills 15 per cent.[17] In this perspective the relatively positive response of Irish industrialists to the survey on the relationship between the education system and their employment needs is understandable. Of those who responded to the question, 65 per cent were satisfied that schools were meeting the needs of industry – of this 65 per cent, 38 per cent believed that the job done by schools was adequate, 26 per cent felt that it was very good and one per cent said that it was excellent. Of the remainder, six per cent felt that there was a lot of room for improvement and 27 per cent saw some room for improvement.[18] Why then is it that employers do not seek a closer articulation between the school curriculum and the world of work?

We must resist the fashionable tendency to attribute the low value placed by employers on vocational relevance to the increasing obsolescence of skills; it is not so much that certain skills have become obsolete but rather that much human effort has been made superfluous by technology. The main reason why employers do not expect schools to provide vocational training is because many vocational skills are acquired on the job rather than in

38

school.[19] Many of the skills necessary to employment, and not just the low level skills of an office cleaner or a factory operative, are most appropriately and also best learned on the job. This applies also to foreign language skills which, perhaps surprisingly, were rated very important by only 26 per cent of employers. Although widely taught in Irish schools, foreign languages are not at all best learned in the classroom context. Rather they are best learned intensively over a short period of time by learners who are motivated by considerations of an immediate and practical nature. [20]

More generally, and specifically with regard to the role of education at second level, the school is quite simply not a suitable arena in which to learn vocational skills. This is because it would be unrealistic to expect schools to teach skills to a degree of specialisation which would be relevant to the workplace. Where specialist training is necessary to do certain jobs such as, for example, performing heart surgery, piloting aircraft, or driving heavy vehicles then the school is not the appropriate institution to provide it. We might also ask what sort of training the school could be expected to provide, for example, to prospective bus drivers without involving wasteful replication of the activity and resources of the training provided by specialised driving schools. Such a project would obviously be impractical. It would also be educationally restrictive for school pupils to spend much of their time learning the skills required of future bus drivers.

Moreover, I am aware of no persuasive evidence which indicates that conferring upon the *school* a direct role in vocational preparation would improve the lot of the unemployed or the underemployed. Even if we were to accept that the school curriculum should be directly related to the world of work, we would require evidence that particular school programmes of training in specific areas could help to secure employment for those unemployed. We would also need evidence pointing to job vacancies unfilled because of specific failures on the school's part to provide relevant training in identifiable areas, as well as evidence to show that there are people now in employment who might perform their jobs better as a result of particular changes of a direct vocational character in the school curriculum. Although little study has been conducted into what is actually learned in schools or on how how long it has been retained, it seems unlikely that people would manage their vocational lives any differently or any better as a consequence of any changes of a direct vocational character to the school curriculum.[21] But, as shall be argued in the final section of this paper, the provision of appropriate preparation for working life might have such an effect.

Besides the prudential arguments, there are also educational reasons for opposing any notion of extending the school's role in the area of vocational training. Firstly, there is the epistemological argument. If the school curriculum were to be directly linked to career aspirations, this would mean that pupils who hope to become carpenters would spend most of their time doing woodwork or that those hoping to become accountants would spend their day studying business-related subjects. Such courses of study would be very limited and limiting but it is at least clear what counts as appropriate activity for aspiring carpenters and accountants. In other cases, it would be much more difficult to determine what would be appropriate vocational subject matter in a school curriculum. Certainly adapting the school curriculum to provide direct training for future solicitors or psychologists would entail great changes in what we expect of such a curriculum. Indeed we could find ourselves in a situation where schools function as university faculties in miniature. So it is best to leave the vocational preparation of lawyers and psychologists to universities and to other institutions for professional training.

And there is also an important socio-political dimension to this argument. As vocational skills are so varied, it would be very difficult to decide which skills should be taught to which pupils. Young people could find themselves making vocational choices before having the opportunity to examine more fully for themselves the possible careers open to them. This would give rise to the danger that pupils would be directed to occupations or levels of occupation which would reinforce class divisions. This is because it is most likely that the children of educated parents would be directed towards the more prestigious and well paid occupations. We could then find that the educational system explicitly endorsing a form of social predestination whereby children find themselves locked into the occupational and social class of their parents.[22] After all, when we hear talk of making the school curriculum more relevant to useful employment, people normally think of skills appropriate to fairly menial employment; it is rarely that they are thinking of the skills of judges or surgeons. This is why Colin Wringe acidly observes that the learning of useful skills of a menial character may indeed be useful, not to those who have to learn them, but rather to those who do not. It is certainly useful for those who become leading figures in the professions, commerce and industry to be able to employ others to do menial tasks.[23]

Such then are the limits of the notion of usefulness as an educational aim. Let us turn now to a consideration of the notion of liberal learning and explore its value as an educational aim.

2. ON LIBERAL LEARNING

The essence of the distinction between useful and liberal learning is that the possible direct or indirect usefulness of liberal learning is not relevant to its nature. The defining characteristic of liberal learning is therefore its concern with the enrichment of the individual. Note, however, that the useful and the liberal are not mutually exclusive categories. The distinction between useful and liberal learning must not be understood to imply that what is useful cannot be educationally enriching and that what is educationally enriching cannot be useful. A person may learn German both for personal satisfaction and also in order to do business with German speaking clients. Likewise, the arts of effective and accurate communication serve not only as a form of preparation for work but also as an important form of personal enrichment. Indeed the paradox of liberal learning is its usefulness to practical living. For example, the understanding of the structure of matter provided by theoretical physics has made possible many of the technical achievements of our civilisation.

Yet the usefulness of the disciplines of liberal learning, of science, history, philosophy, theology, mathematics and literary studies is secondary. The primary purpose of these disciplines or forms of thought is to contribute to our understanding of the divine, human and natural worlds, rather than to produce a result which can be used in the practical world of 'getting and spending'.[24] We can describe these activities as being valuable in themselves which means that the point of these activities lies within themselves, rather than in what they enable us to fabricate. The distinction between practical and explanatory activities remains tenable although the exercise of practical skills is informed by understanding and our achievements in understanding are realised through the exercise of intellectual skills. In other words, the exercise of practical skills requires understanding and achievements in understanding contain a skill factor.

As the formal character of liberal learning is its freedom from considerations of utility, the analogy between engaging in such learning and engaging in a conversation is most appropriate. This is because when we speak of genuine conversation, considerations of utility do not apply. Where considerations of utility do apply, then we are not speaking of genuine conversation but of transactional or instrumental discourse, that is, of discourse where our concern is with the expeditious satisfaction of wants. In respect of genuine conversation, it is not appropriate to ask what it is 'for' because the point of conversation lies within the activity of conversing itself, i.e. in the pleasure, stimulation and enlightenment which it provides.

Liberal learning can also be said to be liberating or emancipatory in that it liberates us from the everyday world of 'getting and spending'. Through such learning young people are offered 'a release from the immediacies, the partialities and the abridgements of the local and contemporary world'.[25] This 'release' constitutes 'an emancipation from the mere "fact of living", from the immediate contingencies of place and time of birth, from the tyranny of the moment and from the servitude of a merely current condition.'[26] By providing a vision of the ultimate values and purposes of human life religious education obviously has a crucial role to play in introducing us to quality of life which lies beyond the mere fact of living.[27] Here I am reminded of a marvellous image offered to me by a student who spoke of the relationship between liberal learning and the school as resembling that between religious practice and a church or place of worship. Through religious practice, as through liberal learning, we are offered a release from our practical concerns and, like worship, the pursuit of learning is normally conducted in an institution which is 'a place apart' from other human institutions.[28] This characterisation of liberal learning was offered as a metaphor but perhaps it has more literal force than I appreciated at the time.

As its non-utilitarian nature provides only a negative characterisation of the notion of liberal learning, we need to ask how such learning might be positively characterised. A positive characterisation would point to the propensity of such learning to provide pleasure or to yield satisfaction to learners. Liberal learning can be synonymously characterised as learning for its own sake which is really a metaphorical way of saying learning for the sake of the learner. It does not mean learning for the sake of learning which, interpreted literally, would be a very odd notion indeed. Learning for the sake of learning means therefore learning for the sake of human beings, i.e., for the sake of personal satisfaction and pleasure. The answer to the question of what makes such learning capable of yielding satisfaction or pleasure to different individuals is partly empirical and will depend on contingent features of the structure of the personality of each individual. The quality of the *eros* , the passion, the love and desire prompted by the pursuit of liberal learning is to a large extent therefore a personal matter. Nevertheless, we can identify certain characteristics of this kind of learning which make it capable of yielding pleasure and satisfaction to learners. In the first place, such learning is indeterminate and capable of offering a permanent and inexhaustible challenge to learners. In other words, the pursuits of liberal learning are of their nature activities of learning. In the second place engaging in such learning is associated with the cultivation of desirable states of mind.

Two objections Before exploring these features of liberal learning in any detail, let me dispose of two common objections made against the notion. The first is the dramatic claim that all knowledge, including the curriculum of liberal learning, is simply an instrument of the vested interests of the rich and powerful in society. What we count as knowledge is not merely influenced, but is actually determined, by what is in the economic interests of the agencies of social and political control. But, as Richard Pring points out, if *all* knowledge were simply a reflection of vested interests, then the claim to this effect would be similarly a reflection of these interests.[29] If the proponent of this determinist argument seeks to attribute a special status to his knowledge claim, then he refutes his proposition that knowledge is a reflection of the vested interests of the rich. If he continues to maintain that all knowledge claims, including his own, are explicable in terms of their connection to socio-economic ends, then it is hard to see how arguments regarding the intrinsic merits, plausibility, or validity of claims to knowledge can be conducted. No enquiry whatsoever is possible unless the participants accept the principle of non-contradiction as being compelling in itself. As Pring explains, questions regarding the validity of human knowledge must be carefully distinguished from questions regarding its genesis. Even if a theory could be constructed which explained the genesis of knowledge in terms of its propensity to serve the interests of the agencies of social and political control, this would not affect the validity of argument conducted within the scientific, historical, or philosophical forms of discourse. [30]

Instrumentalism and liberal learning. A second objection is that the use of educational performance to determine suitability for particular kinds of employment and for further education (what is called the credential effect or exchange value of education) must compromise the character of liberal learning. Now in a society where demand for jobs and for third level places exceeds supply, educational achievement is almost inevitably going to be invested with an exchange value. But it does not follow that the intrusion of external motivation compromises the educational value of all learning conducted in this context. Moreover, it is important to offer to third level colleges, to potential employers and most of all to young people themselves some indication of the relationship between their abilities and their ambitions in the academic sphere. And it is important to have an idea of the relationship between abilities and ambitions. A young person may have ambitions to become a physicist or an historian but if s/he fails every examination in physics or history, then we have to admit that his/her abilities outstrip his/her ambitions. The fact that our ambitions can exceed our abilities is an unfortunate reality of life which it would be silly to deny. It applies in most spheres – people may have ambitions in sport, drama or the arts and may just not have the ability to realise these ambitions. This means only that they lack certain abilities; it does not mean that their worth as human beings has been diminished.

And clearly there will almost unavoidably be a tension inherent in a system which uses academic success as a criterion for vocational selection. On this issue we need hardly go as far as Karl Popper who believes that the demands of such selection have the almost unavoidable result that students will study only for reasons of crude personal ambition rather than out of love for their subjects.[31] Although it would be foolish to deny that this can happen, it is hardly inevitable. There is no doubt that human beings tend to act from multiple motives and that there will be some tension inherent in a system which uses academic success for the instrumental purposes of determining suitability for further education or for employment. But it does not follow that the educational value of all learning conducted in this context is compromised by the intrusion of such external motivation. There is no reason why students studying examinations should not also derive pleasure and satisfaction from their study. And my own experience some twenty years ago as a pupil and since as a teacher suggests to me that many manage to enjoy at least some of their studies.

Liberal learning: its two characteristics. Let us turn now to a more detailed consideration of the two major characteristics of liberal learning. The *first* feature of learning in such areas as science and history, mathematics, philosophy and theology is that it has no terminal point prescribed or prescriptible in advance. There is no

45

point at which we can say that we have finished learning about science and history; in other words, these pursuits involve indeterminate learning. Of their nature science and history are activities of learning; in doing science or history our engagement is actually with learning itself. Moreover, in engaging in these activities, not only is the learning involved inexhaustible, but it also presents itself as a permanent challenge to the learner. To increase one's capacity to participate in a tradition of learning demands sustained and concentrated effort and to succeed in making a personal contribution to such a tradition is the exemplary intellectual achievement. With vocational skills the major task of learning is over once we can use our knowledge in the exercise of the skill but the enquiries which constitute the object of liberal learning always remain activities of learning.

One important objection to the distinction between liberal and useful, in the sense of applied, learning might be raised here. It can be argued that the complex and inexhaustible nature of, as well as the challenge presented by, such theoretical activities as science and history are also features of the research and enquiry associated with, for example, medicine and engineering. No doubt one reply which could be made to this objection is that the pursuit of these latter activities presupposes and depends upon the existence of pure scientific enquiry. As Mary Midgley observes:

> The big, crucial discoveries that have made possible the technical advances of the last two centuries, such as those of Faraday and Clark Maxwell about electricity, have nearly all been made by people who were not actually directing their thoughts to practical applications. [32]

Much of the technology that we find useful in promoting our convenience derives from the discoveries of scientists who were engaged in the pursuit of understanding without regard for its future usefulness. This is of course is the paradoxical usefulness of liberal learning referred to previously.

But this is not to justify the study of science in the liberal sense in

terms of its 'significance in enabling some other activities to re-
solve practical problems'.[33] The pursuits of liberal learning need
not be understood in extrinsic terms, i.e. in terms of the 'implications that they possess for the business of living and so on'.[34] No
one would want to deny the contribution which theoretical
enquiry makes to solving practical problems or the strenuous
nature of the intellectual demands made by research in such practical fields as medicine or engineering. But the significance of
scientific enquiry need not be defined solely or primarily in terms
of its useful consequences. The pursuit of scientific understanding
is also significant in other and richer terms. As well as satisfying
intellectual curiosity, the pursuit of scientific understanding
offers experiences of wonder, rapture and delight and it also provides a context in which rationality and intellectual connoisseurship can be at once exercised and developed. Although the medi-
cal or engineering scientists may also enjoy these satisfact-ions,
their enquiries have a different point from those of the pure scientist. Enquiries of the former kind derive their value from what
they enable us to do, those of the latter kind from what they enable us to understand.

In practice, of course, the distinction between enquiries in pure
and applied science may not be clearcut. A pure physicist may
well become preoccupied with some practical problem in design-
ing a space shuttle, and the designer of a space shuttle may find
herself becoming interested in some purely theoretical aspect of
her work. There is absolutely no reason why research in engineering or medicine should not provide pure as well as applied
knowledge. In principle, however, the point of enquiries in the
applied sciences differs from that of enquiries in pure science.
Unlike the researcher in applied science, the focus of the concern
of the pure scientist is not on the practical applications of her
work. Expressed metaphorically we might say that the theoretical
scientist uses the capital of scientific learning, not to spend it in
the production of some technological device, but rather to re-
invest it in the effort to learn more. [35]

The *second* feature of the disciplines of liberal learning is their
association with desirable states of mind. Acquiring a familiarity

with the traditions of inquiry which it is the concern of liberal learning to promote is also connected with the development of an · understanding of humankind and the world and with the cultivation of those desirable qualities which are related to human rationality. Initiation into the traditions or metaphorical languages of human understanding involves the acquisition not only of understanding, but also of the qualities associated with the possession of intellectual skills or 'connoisseurship' and of the intellectual 'virtues'.[36] Intellectual connoisseurship is expressed in the ability to distinguish between the different answers required by the different questions which we ask of the human and natural world as well as a sensitivity to considerations of relevance, accuracy, economy, elegance, and degrees of conclusiveness in argument. Intellectual virtues include such qualities as open-mindedness, imagination, care, perseverance, patience, concentration, precision, intellectual honesty and modesty. The qualities which make up connoisseurship and virtue are importantly constitutive of what we call mind, although human rationality is certainly not composed exclusively of qualities relating to intellectual life. (Mind is used here to refer not simply to the cognitive sphere of human achievement but to all those qualities which are distinctively human.) Such other characteristically human qualities as considerateness or loyalty may also be developed within the educational community, but it is unlikely that these characteristics are acquired primarily in the school or in the prosecution of intellectual endeavours. This is obviously because young people spend more of their time at home than they do at school; in particular, those significant formative early years of life are spent at home.

Nonetheless, those qualities or states of mind which are acquired through engaging in distinctively educational pursuits are peculiarly valuable in what we call mind or rationality. With standards of achievement distinctively and exclusively their own, science, mathematics, philosophy, and art are not reducible or assimilable to any other activity and they make a unique contribution to the development of rationality. Indeed the understanding which such pursuits promote shapes, alters, and makes more discriminating our very consciousness. This understanding is, therefore, one of the most significant features in our identity as human beings. This human identity, or self-understanding of what it is to be human, emerges in a creative interplay between individuals and the traditions of their cultural inheritance. A vital feature of this understanding derives from contact with distinctively educational pursuits. In particular, it is through an appropriation of the literary and historical languages of our culture that our self-understanding is affirmed and becomes enriched.

It is for this reason, and also because of the range of qualities which engagement in educational pursuits calls upon and develops, that the study of history, literature, science, or philosophy is of greater educational value than engaging in even such a game as chess. Chess is a challenging and intellectually demanding game but the conceptual boundaries of the activity, unlike those of science or history, are prescribed and limited. Of chess we might say, to use the words of Oakeshott , that it does not 'significantly look outside itself'.[37]

This relationship between liberal learning and the cultivation of desirable human qualities points to the epistemological connection between education and personal development, or what is less helpfully called self-realisation. No disjunction exists between the aim of personal development and engagement in those activities which compose the universe of liberal learning. Individuals who are learning to make their own the cultural inheritance, into which education is the initiation, become in this way culturally enriched. It is through this learning that we develop more finely and more comprehensively our human capacities to think, to feel, and to act which is what, if anything, 'self-realisation' means. It is important to remember that, in principle, curriculum design admits no distinction between the aim of personal enrichment and that of acquiring knowledge. This is because individuals who are learning to make their own an area of knowledge become in this way personally enriched. And just as liberal learning has no terminal point, neither is there a terminal point at which human beings can be said to have made the most of themselves. The notion of human development admits of no teleology, the self has

49

no predetermined point at which it can be said to be perfect and to have exhausted all the possibilities of rational development open to it.

Means, ends and liberal learning. Before considering the implications of these arguments for curriculum design, there remains to be addressed one persistent objection to the notion of liberal learning as it has been characterised in this essay. I propose to call this objection the means-ends fallacy. This is the fallacy which views the development of understanding and the acquisition of the intellectual qualities and virtues characteristic of liberal learning as related instrumentally to education.

> I am no foe of 'learning for its own sake', although I happen to think that the term is tossed about a good deal as an intrinsic educational good, but rarely examined for meaning. Considered seriously, the notion poses problems. Learning seems to me to be perfectly instrumental, to be invariably for the sake of something else: reward, promotion, amusement, mastery. Different souls learn things for different ends, and some ends are undoubtedly nobler than others, but learning itself is never the end. [38]

It is is also the view which underlies the following observations of F.W. Garforth:

> Education is essentially instrumental; it is not an end in itself but a means both to fulfilment in the individual and to stability and progress in society. It is a tool to achieve the aims which society sets before itself. [39]

More surprisingly in their philosophically sophisticated article, I.M.M. Gregory and R.G. Woods make a similar point. In discussing the status of claims which ascribe intrinsic value to certain educational pursuits, they suggest that this may be a way of talking about the effects of such activities in developing certain desirable personal characteristics. Thus, for example:

> Talking about the study of English literature being valuable in itself is a way of saying that this study may be instrumental in the creating of persons who are sensitive, imaginative, affectively well balanced and so on. [40]

However, we can no more apply a means-ends model to the benefits which attend liberal learning than we can speak of the activity of sailing as a means to the pleasurable end of enjoyment. The exhilaration, the sense of mastery, well-being and closeness to nature which a person gets from sailing are not ends to which certain physical arrangements are the means. From point of view of enthusiastic and practised participants, such feelings are what sailing is for them; the feelings are not ends which are instrumentally related to participation in the activity itself. Similarly, for example, feelings of increased sympathy towards others, an understanding of, and a sense of outrage at, social injustice are not effects, results, or consequences which may or may not follow a sensitive reading of Dickens's *Hard Times*. Reading and responding to the novel actually means having these and similar experiences. They are emergent characteristics of the experience of reading Dickens – which is not, of course, to suggest that all readers will respond in the same way or have the same kinds of experiences. Accordingly initiation into distinctively educational activities entails the development of understanding and of particular rational qualities as a feature, rather than as an effect or result, of the pursuit of these activities. Education consists in engaging in activities, it is not a by-product of engaging in them.

Nor must the achievement of understanding and the acquisition of these desirable human qualities be conceived as slightly different extrinsic ends to education. To speak of these as extrinsic ends is like speaking of pleasure and stimulation as extrinsic ends of conversation. Personal enrichment is not an end at all; it is part of what being educated means. To describe an educational activity as valuable in itself or as worth pursuing for its own sake is not, therefore, to ascribe to it a status independent of what it contributes to enabling us to live fuller and richer lives. Rather it is to point to its propensity to enrich the lives of those who accept the invitation to acquire facility in the metaphorical language in which it consists and to join in the conversation to which it lends its voice.

At this point it is appropriate to consider the implications of these arguments for the design of the school curriculum.

3. USEFULNESS, LIBERAL LEARNING
AND THE SCHOOL CURRICULUM

Now here let me stress that the argument of this essay does not imply that what is learned in school should bear no direct relation to the world of work. Of course it should. But what we need are not courses of putative vocational utility but practical and imaginatively conceived courses of preparation for working life.[41] There is evidence to suggest such preparation, rather than vocational training, is in fact what employers actually want of schools. And it is this kind of preparation for work which is being sought by the young people who complain about the lack of such preparation in school.[42] Such preparation needs little justification and, even on a narrow account of schooling as initiation into a cultural inheritance, this aspect of education is defensible. Part of understanding a culture involves understanding how wealth is created and how industry and the world of work in general are organised. Such understanding might also serve to promote more informed and fulfilling participation by young people in their future work. Careers Education is another essential part of preparation for working life as no single family or community agency could be expected to provide systematic and structured instruction in the range of career possibilities open to young people. Education in Trade Unionism would also be part of a programme of preparation for working life as it can help to prepare pupils for their future role as workers and also serve to develop their sense of community responsibility. And in the context of a future with increasing likelihood of enforced idleness through redundancy and shortened working hours, educators must address the important need to develop in young people resources – what Jane Austen calls 'resources for solitude' – in order to make creative use of their leisure time.[43]

Another important practical way in which schools can contribute to preparing young people for the world of work is by teaching the skills of effective communication. (Awareness of the importance of this this aspect of education is indeed one of the positive features of the the new Junior Certificate.) Because of the importance of the skills of accurate and effective communication in the workplace, more specific and systematic attention must be paid to teaching the mechanics of oral and written communication to all pupils.[44] (At present remedial classes enjoy the benefit of such attention.) In school, therefore, learning to compose proper letters of application and *curricula vitae* and to perform other practical tasks in written communication is of obvious importance. So also is learning the techniques of good self-presentation, not only at interviews but in general social situations. It is important for young people to be taught how their speech and deportment convey to others an impression of their whole personalities. Improving the way they project themselves will prove of great assistance to young people in their vocational and personal lives.

But it is through what I call the curriculum of liberal learning that the school best prepares young people for the world of work. (This is not to claim that liberal learning is to be justified on account of its usefulness in this regard.) It is through such a curriculum that young people are most likely to reap the practical benefits of education. In spite of fashionable demands for 'relevance' in the school curriculum, we have seen that evidence continues to confirm that what employers value most highly is a general education, together with the skills of accurate and effective communication and appropriate personal qualities. This means that in preparing young people for the world of work, the curriculum of liberal learning (which is what is meant by 'general education') is centrally relevant. Accordingly the appropriate contribution of school to the world of work is best conceived as an indirect one.

Much of this indirect preparation is, of course, at present and quite rightly, undertaken in schools. Woodwork, metalwork, technical drawing, and building construction are obvious examples of skills currently taught in schools which may prove of vocational usefulness. In so far as the study of maths and science is necessary for careers in medicine or engineering, their presence in the school curriculum has a vocational import. Indeed future scientists and historians, while at school, are directly engaged in apprencticeship to these careers in their study of science and history. But the justification for the inclusion in the school curriculum of any of the above subjects is not primarily vocational and their potential vocational usefulness is not the principal reason for teaching them. The real justification for teaching these subjects is different – and derives from the fact that it is through the learning of these subjects that pupils both acquire certain worthwhile skills and come to develop their understanding in ways which are satisfying and enriching.

But, as we have seen, employers lay greatest emphasis on the qualities of character of their prospective employees, so let us recall some of the personal qualities which can be developed through the curriculum of liberal learning. Among such qualities are as open-mindedness, imagination, care, perseverance, concentration, precision, intellectual honesty, and modesty as well as a sensitivity to considerations of relevance, accuracy, economy, elegance and degrees of conclusiveness in argument. Unfortunately the tradition of liberal learning has not been sufficiently associated with the cultivation of critical thinking and with the promotion of such valued qualities as resourcefulness, initiative, and willingness to co-operate with others but there is no good reason why, in principle, it should not also serve these purposes. [45]

And here it is necessary to emphasise that the forementioned practical activities of woodwork, metalwork, as well as other craftwork also have a place in the curriculum of liberal learning. Craftwork has an ambivalent status in that it is situated at the interface between the worlds of practical and aesthetic experience. Although useful in the sense of requiring manual skill (see Part One of this article), practical activities also have an aesthetic character. The desire to create an object of beauty can prompt an individual to produce a work of art in wood or metal. Because certain pursuits often have a practical as well as an aesthetic function does not exclude them from the curriculum of liberal learning. Certainly these activities offer intellectual challenge and engagement in them can make profound demands of human creativity. And in common with theoretical activities, practical pursuits offer a context for the exercise and cultivation of such qualities as concentration, willingness to take pains, and perseverance. Moreover, as Patrick Walsh argues, to such intellectual virtues as fairmindedness, honesty, and clarity which are characteristic of theoretical pursuits, there correspond 'effectiveness, economy and good workmanship as virtues of practical activities'.[46] And these too are distinctively human or rational qualities or virtues.

Yet one can recognise the rationality in every episode of distinctively human conduct, from tying one's shoe lace to solving a problem in nuclear physics and still assign a primacy to theoretical pursuits over practical activities. The reason for assigning to theoretical pursuits such a primacy is because they have a more intimate connection with human understanding and consequently with human identity. Literary and historical studies, in particular, make a vital contribution to the development of human self-understanding. This does not mean that educational value should be attached to theoretical pursuits alone, or that such pursuits should invariably enjoy curricular priority. To some young people practical activities may offer the most appropriate vehicle for creative expression, and to others these activities may represent the only area in which they can engage in significant self-expression.

Whatever form the curriculum of liberal learning takes for individual pupils, it is through such a curriculum that we best serve human and practical needs of our young people. Before equipping young people with vocational skills, education must foster in them an ability to make 'considered choices'.[47] In order to respond constructively to programmes of vocational training, young people need an education which endows them with a vision of the worthwhile in human life. And it is a curriculum of liberal learning which will enable young people to develop this vision.

In developing a vision of the worthwhile in human life, religious education has a central role to play. In its sensitivity to the dignity and preciousness of the human person, religious education has a unique potential to help young people to live more fully and more richly. The knowledge and understanding acquired in other subjects can be drawn together in religion class to enable students to develop a holistic vision of life. In religion class, young people are given an opportunity to explore further some of the profound metaphysical and ethical questions about our nature, purpose and responsibility which may arise in the teaching of other subjects. Not only is religious education perfectly consistent with the essential purposes of liberal learning but no subject is more likely to contribute to the humane, spiritual and civilising purposes which characterise the pursuit of such learning.

Acknowledgement: For sharing with me his vision of essential educational values and of the limits of vocationalism in education and for prompting me to write about the subject, I am indebted to my late brother, Aidan.

Notes:

1   In Kevin Williams, 'Tradition and Fashion in Curriculum Design', *Oideas*, 31 (Fomhar,1987), pp.66-76 this trend is examined in some detail. This spirit of utilitarian thinking is not, of course, peculiar to Ireland. The British versions of such thinking are explored in such books as Charles Bailey, *Beyond the Present and the Particular* (London: Routledge and Kegan Paul, 1984) and Colin Wringe, *Understanding Educational Aims* (London: Unwin Hyman, 1988).

2   Mary Midgley, 'The Use and Uselessness of Learning', *European Journal of Education*, Vol. 25, No. 3, 1990. pp. 283-294, p. 292.

3   Francis Dunlop, 'Review Article: The Rational-Liberal Neglect of Human Nature', *The Journal of Philosophy of Education*, Vol. 25, No. 1 (1991), pp.109-119, p. 111.

4   See Confederation of Irish Industry, *CII Newsletter: Confederation of Irish Industry*, 'Human Resources – the key issues',Vol. 53, No. 9 (10 July 1990), pp. 2-4. The figures are given later in this article. An analysis of this report can be found in C. Murphy, 'School Leavers Ill-Equipped for Work', *Working and Living: A Supplement to The Irish Times*, 10 August 1990.

5   See FAS Information Services, 'Few Skill Shortages in Ireland: Major FAS report reveals', *FAS, Training and Employment News*, November, 1991.

6   For examples of this view see C. Bailey, *Beyond the Present and the Particular* , pp. 163-192 and K.Williams, 'Tradition and Fashion in Curriculum Design' and also Ruth Johnathan, 'The Manpower Service Model of Education', *Cambridge Journal of Education*, Vol. 13, No. 2 (1983), pp.3-10. For a recent expression of the viewsee Finola Kennedy, 'Belief that education system does not cater for all echoed', *The Irish Times*, 1/2 January 1992, p.12, and the published report of the Industrial Policy Review Group (January, 1992).

7   The spirit of current, utilitarian assumptions regarding the teaching of foreign languages is communicated in the following two 'Commentary' pieces: Ray Bowman, 'Room for improvement', *Working and Living: A Supplement to The Irish Times*, 1 June 1990, p. 12 and Gemma Hussey, 'The gift of languages', Ibid. 22 June 1990, p.12. The point is also raised by the C.I.I. in 'Human Resources – the key issues', p.3.

8   Christina Murphy analyses this trend in an interesting article, 'RTC choices mirror universities', *The Irish Times*, 20 February 1991, p.8.

9   See the *Statistical Reports* provided annually by the Department of Education. This trend is analysed in Kathleen Lynch, 'Education and the Paid Labour Market: A Comment on the Issue of Relevance', *Irish Educational Studies*, Vol. 11 (1992) (forthcoming).

10   See John Vaizey, 'The School in Question: an economist's viewpoint', *Oxford Review of Education*, Vol. 5, No. 3, pp.207-214.

11   See Roger Dale and Eurico Pires, 'Linking People and Jobs: the indeterminate place of educational credentials', in *Selection, Certification and Control: Social Issues in Educational Assessment*, ed. Patricia Broadfoot (London and New York: The Falmer Press, 1984).

12   See Central Statistics Office, *Labour Force Survey 1989*, (Government Publications: Dublin,1990), Table 8, p. 24 and Central Statistics Office, *Census of Population 1981* (Government Publications: Dublin,1990), Vol. 4, pp. 150-157.

13   See K. Lynch, 'Education and the Paid Labour Market'. For references and analysis of empirical research in this section, I am indebted to this fine article by Kathleen Lynch.

14   See I. Berg, *Education and Jobs* (New York: Praeger, 1970), pp. 85-104, 143-176. And J. Oxenham reports on a study by a multinational firm which found the difference in managerial skills between graduate and non-graduate staff to be insignificant. See J. Oxenham, 'Employers, Jobs and Qualifications' in *Education Versus Qualifications*, ed. J. Oxenham (London: Allen and Unwin, 1984), p.60.

15   See C.I.I., 'Human Resources – the key issues', p.1.

16   This argument of Sir Douglas Hague, chairman of Metapraxis, the information technology management consultancy can be found in an article by Sarah Johnson, 'I think, therefore I learn', in *The Daily Telegraph*, 15 March, 1990. Among research findings in this area see, for example, R. Dale and E. Pires, 'Linking People and Jobs: the indeterminate place of educational credentials'; J. Oxenham, 'Employers, Jobs and Qualifications', pp. 74-76 and W. W. Wilms, 'Captured by the American Dream: Vocational Education in the

United States' in *Vocationalizing Education*, eds. J. Lauglo and K. Lillis (Oxford: Pergamon Press, 1988), pp. 81-93. For a review of relevant research see K. Lynch, 'Education and the Paid Labour Market'.

17 See C.I.I., 'Human Resources – the key issues', p.1, and also H. J. Noah and M. A. Eckstein, 'Business and Industry Involvement with Education in Britain, France and Germany', in J. Lauglo and K. Lillis, eds.*Vocationalizing Education*.

18 See C.I.I., 'Human Resources – the key issues', Figure 4, p.4.

19 See, for example, R. Collins, *The Credential Society* (New York: Academic Press, 1979), p. 17.

20 See Eric Hawkins, *Modern Languages in the School Curriculum* (Cambridge: Cambridge University Press, 1987), p.190. See also K. Williams, 'Languages in Schools: the limits of utility', *Oideas*, 37 (Fomhar, 1991), pp.112-119.

21 A recent Irish publication provides some interesting research in this area. See D.F. Hannan and S. Shorthall, The Quality of *Their Education: School Leavers' Views of Educational Objectives and Outcomes*, Paper 153, (Dublin: The Economic and Social Research Institute, 1991).

22 Colin Wringe draws on the work of John Dewey to elaborate on this theme in C. Wringe, *Understanding Educational Aims*, pp.55-71.

23 Ibid., p. 66.

24 This phrase is taken from Wordsworth's poem, 'The World Is Too Much With Us', *Oxford Anthology of English Literature: Romantic Poetry and Prose* (Oxford: Oxford University Press, 1973).

25 This quotation is taken from Michael Oakeshott, 'Education: The Engagement and Its Frustration' in T. Fuller, ed., *The Voice of Liberal Learning: Michael Oakeshott on Education* (New Haven/London, Yale University Press, 1989), p. 86.

26 Ibid., p. 93.

27 Here I have slightly adapted a sentence from A.N. Whitehead, *Religion in the Making* (Cambridge: Cambridge University Press, 1926), p.80.

28 This phrase is taken from M. Oakeshott, 'Education: The Engagement and Its Frustration', pp. 69, 71, 72, 76.

29 R. Pring, 'Knowledge out of Control', in Michael Golby, Jane Greenwald and Ruth West, ed., *Curriculum Design* (London: Croom Helm/The Open University Press), pp.128-137.

30 Ibid.

31 K. Popper, *The Open Society and its Enemies* (London: Routledge and Kegan Paul, 1966), pp.135-136.

32 M. Midgley, 'The Use and Uselessness of Learning' p. 291.

33   I. M.M. Gregory and R.G. Woods, 'Valuable in Itself', *Educational Philosophy and Theory*, Vol. 3, No. 2 (October, 1971), pp.51-64, p.62

34   Ibid., p.61.

35   These metaphors are adapted from M. Oakeshott, *Rationalism in Politics and Other Essays* (London: Methuen, 1981), pp. 307-311.

36   See M. Oakeshott, 'Learning and Teaching' in T. Fuller, ed., *The Voice of Liberal Learning: Michael Oakeshott on Education*, p.60.

37   M. Oakeshott, *Rationalism in Politics*, p.308.

38   Richard A. Hawley, *The Headmaster's Papers* (New York: Bantam Books, 1984), p.121.

39   F. W. Garforth, 'Values in Society and Education', *Education for Teaching* , No. 64 (May 1964), p.25.

40   I.M.M. Gregory and R.G. Woods, 'Valuable in Itself', p. 59.

41   An account of such a course can be found in K. Williams and G.McNamara, *The Vocational Preparation Course: An Educational Appraisal and Practical Guide* (Dublin: Cumann na Meanmhúinteoirí, Éire, 1985), pp. 79-98.

42   See C.I.I., 'Human Resources – the key issues', pp. 2/3. For an account of the attitudes of young people to the need for preparation for work see D.F. Hannan and S. Shorthall, *The Quality of Their Education: School Leavers' Views of Educational Objectives and Outcomes*, ch. 5.

43   Jane Austen, *Persuasion* (Harmondsworth: Penguin, 1973), p. 64.

44   See C.I.I., 'Human Resources – the key issues', p.1.

45   In K. Williams, 'Tradition and Fashion in Curriculum Design', and in K. Williams, 'The Classical Idiom in Curriculum Design', *Curriculum*, Vol. 11, No.3 (1990), pp. 132-139 and 'The Gift of an Interval', *British Journal of Educational Studies*, Vol. 37, No. 4 (Nov.1989), pp. 384-398, I have attempted to indicate how liberal learning might be conceptualised and presented in these terms.

46   P. D. Walsh, 'The Upgrading of Practical Subjects', *Journal of Further and Higher Education*, 2, pp.58-71, p.61.

47   See R. Jonathan, 'The Manpower Service Model of Education', p. 6.

III. Irish Educational Policy in a Philosophical perspective: The Legacy of Liberalism

Eoin Cassidy

1. THE EDUCATION ACT AND A PHILOSOPHY OF EDUCATION

1. 1 The reluctance of successive governments to articulate a philosophy of education

In an introduction to the summer edition of the educational journal *Decision Maker*, an issue devoted to the proposed GreenPaper on Education, the then Minister for Education, Mary O'Rourke, stated it was her intention that the Green Paper

> ... will cover all aspects of education : setting out our basic educational philosophy, together with goals, policies and strategies for implementation of these goals. [1]

This statement of intent to set out a basic educational philosophy is one which will be welcomed by educators including many who, in contributions to that same issue of *Decision Maker*, advocated such a commitment and who have all highlighted the fact that, in the Ireland of the late twentieth century the lack of a clear statement of the philosophy underlying educational policy is increasingly unsustainable.[2]

The significance of this commitment by the former Minister to set out a basic philosophy of education must be seen in the context of a marked reluctance on the part of successive Government and the various bodies which in recent years have been commissioned with the task of curriculum reform to engage in this type of reflective analysis.[3] Apart from the explicit reference in the *Programme for Action in Education (1984-1987)* that 'the programme does *not* propose to set out a philosophy of education',[4] the reluctance to address in any systematic fashion this most fundamental issue is something which also marks the two major consultative documents from the Curriculum and Examinations Board which were published in the 1980's, namely the *Issues and Structure in Education* (1984) and *Senior Cycle: Development and Direction* (1986). The first tentative steps to redress this imbalance are to be seen in the *Guide to the Junior Certificate*, published by the National Council for Curriculum and Assessment in 1989.[5] It is, however, only with the publication by the N.C.C.A. in June 1991 of two position papers that this critical lacuna in previous publications was adverted to, and the importance of a philosophy of education was recognized. The position paper, *The Curriculum at Junior Level*, 1,3, contains the following statement:

> There have been criticisms of Irish curriculum provision insofar as the aims, objectives and overall educational philosophy and thrust have often been implicit, rather than explicitly stated. The Junior Certificate programme in its similar specifications in respect of individual syllabuses, has already begun to address these weaknesses. [6]

The position paper entitled *The Curriculum at Senior Level*, Section 2:3 contains the following:

> Arising from the consultative process to date, it is clear that there is general agreement on:
> * the need for a fuller statement of the philosophical basis for education at that level and for a greater emphasis on its moral and spiritual dimensions.

1.2   The importance of a philosophical statement

How important is this issue? If one values the coherence of a school's curriculum the issue is of enormous importance. A philosophy of education is an expression of how one understands education. The aims of education, the shape of the curriculum, even the methods of teaching, ultimately find their justification in terms of the particular philosophy that guides one's deliberations. Furthermore, it is not just the explicit curriculum that is shaped by the underlying philosophy, but also all the choices which one makes about education including, perhaps most importantly of all, the choices concerning the implicit or hidden curriculum that is commonly called the school ethos – that belief structure and/or environmental context within which all learning takes place. If the importance of the school ethos in the educational process is being increasingly recognized today, it is also a fact that more and more educators are becoming aware of how vulnerable the school ethos is to shifts in the prevailing philosophy of education. A graphic illustration of this was to be seen in the hostile reaction of many school principals to the *Sunday Tribune* article of 6th October 1991[8] which attempted to grade schools in terms of examination results. If it is true, as Dr Joseph Dunne of St Patrick's College, Drumcondra in a recent article suggests[9] that it is the ethos which is perhaps the real thing which is learnt after subjects have been forgotten, then it is not surprising that school principles objected to the attempt to evaluate schools from this narrow perspective.

The need for society not only to have, but to clearly articulate a philosophy of education is further underlined when one recognizes that in the absence of an explicit philosophy, the agenda for education policy will be set by the economic forces of supply and demand. Nature abhors a vacuum and the market will provide, or what many educators are only too acutely aware, the market has already provided, the philosophical context or the 'working' theoretical model for Irish education. It is not even as if the absence of an agreed philosophy has left room for a genuine pluralism. What is increasingly recognized or feared, depending on one's point of view, is that the philosophical agenda for Irish education today is one that is increasingly influenced by a narrow economic pragmatism. It is undoubtedly a sensitivity to this reality and a desire to bring this often concealed agenda into the public forum that accounts for the increasing number of voices who are calling for a public debate on the type of philosophy or philosophies of education which would be acceptable to Irish society.

1.3 *Explaining the reluctance to articulate a philosophy of education*

How does one explain the reluctance of successive Governments to engage in such a fundamental debate on the philosophy underlying the structure of education? There are a number of fairly plausible reasons why, in the early years of the State, Governments would have thought it wise to refrain from such an important intervention. These reasons have much to do with the then recent memories of the rather sharp controversies between the Catholic hierarchy and the British administration which attempted during the years 1919/20 to steer through Parliament an Education Act. Although mainly restricted to the issue of control of schools, these controversies would certainly go some way to explain the marked reluctance of the State in the early years after independence to initiate the type of debate required in order to develop a philosophy of education. It may also be as Dr Barrington in an article states 'in a peasant society it does not pay to philosophize in public.'[10] However, the answer is more likely to be found in the fact that until quite recently Irish society was remarkably homogeneous. In such a society it was probably felt to be unnecessary to state the obvious.

Today, the reason for this reluctance to state a clear philosophy of education may also lie in the belief that it is unnecessary – but unnecessary from a totally different and less benign perspective. In this scenario there would be no need for the State to impose a philosophy of education because the market forces will ensure that a philosophy geared to the needs of economic pragmatism will prevail and that it is precisely this agenda which underlies the State's commitment to education. In this context it would obviously suit the State to appear both to have relatively little control over the education system and also to suggest that it is neutral vis-à-vis various and sometimes conflicting philosophies of education. Lest this viewpoint appear somewhat fanciful one ought to be aware of the publication by Kathleen Lynch, University College, Dublin, which seeks to substantiate that thesis. [11]

I am not however persuaded by this rather Machiavellian scenario and tend to think that there is a more plausible reason to explain the recent reluctance of the State to involve itself in issues relating to a philosophy of education.

The perspective which I will be suggesting is one which places recent Irish education thinking firmly in the context of main-stream liberalism, that political culture which, as the name suggests, provides the theoretical basis for modern liberal democracy and which, in turn, is the chosen model for societal living by the majority of what is loosely called the developed world. In this context, the reluctance to set out a basic philosophy of education is based on a number of interrelated factors. Firstly, there is the perception of the difficulty of securing consensus as to what such a philosophy statement should contain. Secondly, there is the view that a modern liberal democracy should, if not encourage, at least tolerate pluralism. The belief is that a liberal democracy in contrast to various forms of totalitarianism, ought not to impose too rigid a view regarding the nature and purpose of education and that the maximum amount of freedom should be left to citizens – in this case parents – to decide on the type of education best suited to the needs of their children. These reasons have to do with how one understands the role of the State. In modern liberal democracies individual freedom is perceived as a core value and the consequent pluralism must be protected insofar as possible.

In what follows I propose to examine the main features of liberalism in order both to discern some of the cultural influences on Irish education policy and to propose a re-commitment to certain values neglected in a liberalist ethos.

2. LIBERALISM AND A PHILOSOPHY OF EDUCATION

2. 1 *Liberalism and the spirit of the enlightenment*
A difficulty which attends the study of any concept as broad as that suggested by the word liberalism is that it tends to be open to as many interpretations as there are interpreters. This is inevitably the case with most 'isms'. They are umbrella terms designed to express a certain ethos or cluster of values. The difficulty of defining a tradition such as liberalism is also bound up with the fact that tradition constantly modifies itself in terms of the history of its own development and, finally, there is always the critical distinction between the theory and practice of a tradition. These considerations make one hesitate in persisting with such a term which is so capable of being misunderstood. Liberalism does,

however, offer a privileged insight into the character of the cultural values which have produced our so called 'Western' society or modern liberal democracy. I do not wish to say that our contemporary culture is exclusively liberal, just as I do not wish to be accused of neglecting the formative influence of other traditions. My point is, however, that the term liberalism uniquely describes many of the dominant values of contemporary society and describes them in a way that allows us to trace the origins of much of our culture to the emergence of that movement in the seventeenth century commonly designated as the enlightenment.[12] At the core of the liberal ethos is a respect for human autonomy, in particular, the rights associated with the belief in the freedom and equality of each person. In addition, liberalism embraces many values, all of them closely interrelated. These values include tolerance, pluralism, individual autonomy, a commitment to scientific rationality, equality of persons and liberal democracy. Translated into the sphere of contemporary education policy the positive effects of this liberalist ethos can be seen in the commitment, at least in theory, to equality of opportunity and respect for the freedom/ individuality of every child. Specifically a liberalist ethos in education would eschew all forms of indoctrination, authoritarianism and elitism.

Liberalism as a political doctrine incorporating a highly developed theory of the person, emerged over a relatively lengthy period of history and in distinct phases, the earliest of which is most commonly dated to the philosophical revolution inaugurated by Descartes in the seventeenth century. The development of post modernist philosophy in the latter half of this century with its rejection of the possibility of objectivity, may in time be perceived as the final celebration of liberalism.

(a) The emergence of scientific rationality. In its earliest phase, liberalism is expressed in the context of the emergence of the autonomous subject, and in the parallel assertion of the dignity of scientific rationality in opposition to all forms of authority, tradition or belief structures. Influenced by the emergence of the 'new' scientific methodology, and in turn providing a powerful impetus to

the development of modern culture, this expression of liberalism – the autonomous reason shorn of all contact with history and culture – was to give rise directly to a form of scientific positivism in which undue respect was accorded to the supposed neutral and objective status of scientific research. The effects of this form of positivism are unfortunately still to be seen in influential writings on education published as recently as 1970. [13]

(b) The emergence of the individual qua *individual.* The proclamation of the autonomy of the human reason and the autonomy of the human subject are the twin pillars of the early phase of the liberal enlightenment. If the writings of Descartes and Kant are most closely associated with the former, the names of the English philosophers Locke and Hobbes are those linked to the emergence of the autonomy of the human subject or, as is recognized today, the emergence for the first time in history of philosophy of the individual *qua* individual. In marked contrast to the whole of classical and medieval culture where the individual was consistently defined in the context of a recognition of the essentially social character of human nature, liberalism celebrated the birth, not just of the individual, but of individualism, and individualism as a political doctrine. Through the writings principally of Rousseau and Voltaire in France, this development of liberalism in turn influenced the framing of the American constitution and the subsequent development of a large scale acceptance in the nineteenth and twentieth centuries of the ideal of liberal democracy, one founded on the notion of the individual *qua* individual and differing fundamentally from the earlier classic expression of democracy which was based on the idea of the *polis* and the shared destiny of individuals not as individuals but as members of the *polis* or community.

(c) The emergence of a pluralist culture. If the origins of liberalism can be traced to the emergence of the autonomous *cogito* of scientific rationality and the rise of modern individualism it must be recognized that liberalism also developed in the context of the break-up of an older world view – the dissolution of the inherited sources of meaning that gave a coherence and a unity to the medieval and early Renaissance cultures. The loss of scholastic meta-

physics and the effect of the Reformation on the unity of culture and Christendom shaped in no uncertain manner the emerging liberal culture. Despite the development of scientific rationality which offered, albeit temporarily, the possibility of a new unified world view, liberalism, from as early as the eighteenth century, took the form of a doctrine structured to provide a way of coping with irresolvable conflict. In this context two core features of liberalism emerged. namely, tolerance and a belief in the value of, or an acceptance of, pluralism. Liberal democracy is the first political experiment which was not only designed to respect the values of freedom and equality, but primarily sought to promote tolerance and to accommodate, insofar as was practical, a pluralism of values, ideals, religious beliefs, etc.

The most recent expression of this feature of liberalism, and one whose importance should not be underestimated for understanding current (mainly British) writings on the philosophy of education, is the rejection in our century of the logical positivist tradition and its replacement by what is loosely called analytical philosophy. Logical positivism was the last theoretical attempt to justify scientific positivism. Its abandonment by Wittgenstein heralded the emergence of a philosophical tradition that still has enormous influence today – that of linguistic analysis. Briefly stated, it is a system that embraced pluralism in its most extreme form and literally abandoned the concern for truth in favour of a concern for meaning, or more precisely, it declared that truth is a function of belief rather than *vice versa*. While recognizing the complex dialectical relationship between structures of belief and truth, it must be understood that the philosophical tradition which remains faithful to the writings of the later Wittgenstein, and that includes no small portion of contemporary philosophers of education, embraces a pluralism that is defined in terms of relativism, the rejection of the objectivity of truth or value. In fact the contemporary preoccupation with analytic philosophy reveals, not only that liberalism in its extreme form is inseparable from relativism or at best perspectivism, but it equally shows how important the liberal agenda is for understanding our contemporary philosophical culture and, more specifically, contemporary philosophy of education. [14]

(d) Liberalism and the emergence of the pragmatist. If liberalism has its origins in the context of a recognition of the inevitability and ultimately the unresolvability of conflict, liberalism as a political theory could not espouse unrestricted pluralism which would be a recipe for anarchy. Consequently, in the course of its development there have been many attempts to construct some harmonious basis for social interaction. In practice, liberal democracy has tended to embrace an amalgam of two different and in many cases conflicting theories, namely, contractarianism and utilitarianism, the former associated with philosophers such as Kant, Locke and Rousseau, the latter made famous largely through the writings of Hume and Bentham and more importantly today, through the legacy of writings of the economist Adam Smith. Both of these theories are classical expressions of liberalism or of the liberal dilemma of how to order a society where there exists no shared vision of the good or *télos* of human nature. Contractarianism gives prominence to the notion of rights. In John Rawls' contemporary exposé of contractarianism it is the rights of freedom and equality in that order which are primary. Utilitarianism bases its theory of social justice on various expressions of the idea of utility. Contractarianism is more genuinely liberal in that it suggests that certain individual rights are inviolable and it attempts to avoid any commitment to a shared notion of the good. Utilitarianism in some respects marks the abandonment or the modification of liberalism in favour of a pragmatic theory of the good, variously defined as pleasure or utility and more recently in more straightforward consumerist terms. In contrast to contractarianism, utilitarianism involves an instrumentalist conception of the person because in the last analysis the freedom and equality of individuals is sacrificed for the sake of maximizing utility or, more accurately today, the maximizing of consumer goods or *per capita* gross national product. However, it is not only in a contemporary utilitarian ethos that the economic agenda takes precedence. The most influential contemporary contractarian, John Rawls, has his own theory of the good albeit as he says a thin theory of the good.[15] The decision as to what rights are inviolable and which rights get precedence depends upon some theory of the goal or goals which are universally desired. In the last analysis, John Rawls' thin theory of the good is an economic one. Consequently, it is economic

pragmatism which provides the working agenda of contemporary liberalism, a pragmatism which in the end ironically destroys the genuine pluralism upon which liberalism was founded.

2. 2 *The legacy of liberalism and its effect on education policy: An Introduction*

As it has been outlined, the legacy of liberalism is not universally positive, and that notwithstanding the contribution which it has made to the emergence of a scientific rationality and liberal democracy, the emphasis on human rights and the contemporary commitment to a more tolerant society. In what follows I will be highlighting some negative features of liberalism and their effect on current education policy in Ireland. In doing so I do not wish my comments to be construed as a desire to reject in summary fashion the culture of liberalism. They are presented so that the influences affecting the formation of Irish education policy would be better understood.

(a) Liberalism and scientific rationality. The most damaging legacy of liberalism is the encouragement of the belief that truth is ahistorical. Apart from the fact that this vision of truth, if translated into education policy, would obviously undermine the value of history as a subject, it would also have serious implications for the way in which languages are taught. The acquiring of a technical competence in language skills, apart from a sensitivity to the cultural heritage expressed through language, would result in a fairly drastic impoverishment of the students' experience. The divorce between fact and value or between the 'is' and 'ought' which is the essence of scientific positivism and which was a core principle of much English language philosophy for the last hundred years could have had, and still might have, major implications for the status of religious and/or moral education on the school curriculum.

The dominance of scientific rationality has the potential to lead to an unquestioned prioritizing of the technical at the expense of any other subjects on the curriculum. It also leaves the way open to an intellectual elitism in school which would have the effect of grossly undervaluing the potential and the dignity of the intellectually less well endowed student.

(b) Liberalism and individualism. An individualist ethos is by its very nature a competitive ethos. It is also one which places very little, if any, value on the interpersonal character of human existence – the value of friendship, partnership and mutual support. There is little doubt that the individualist culture which we have inherited is a factor in the dominant place in our education system which is presently accorded to the examination system. The possibility of overcoming or countering a system which produces losers as well as winners is directly related to that of creating an ethos which gives primacy to the relational/interpersonal dimension of human nature.

(c) Liberalism and the emergence of pluralism. Pluralism can be based on a desire to promote a tolerant environment and to that extent it can have a very positive effect in countering the prejudices which all to a lesser or greater extent are subject. However, the unquestioned espousal of pluralism more often than not clearly implies the rejection of the very notion of objective truth. The dangers of encouraging a school environment in which moral values are seen to be subjective and relative needs little elaboration. However, it is equally important to note that an environment which links in an unquestioning manner the teaching of objective moral truth with indoctrination or one which assumes that moral education can be equated with value clarification in the way in which liberal analytic philosophy has jettisoned truth in favour of meaning is one which has potentially very serious implications for education.

(d) Liberalism and the emergence of pragmatism. Liberalism is pluralistic in theory but pragmatic in practice, and there is nothing more pragmatic in contemporary liberalism than the economic agenda of consumerism. In a consumer culture the equality of opportunity which education cherishes as an ideal is constantly in danger of being sacrificed on the altar of economic priorities. The market forces which determine so much of contemporary life do not leave the education system unscathed. Indeed the recent publication from the Economic and Social Research Institute entitled *The Quality of their Education* which assesses school-leavers' views of educational objectives and outcomes makes very sober reading.

70

The narrow economic agenda overshadows almost all other considerations.[16] A similar perspective can be gleaned from an article entitled 'Education Goes to Market' by Leslie Bash, which forms part of a publication commenting on the recent Education Reform Act in the United Kingdom.[17] An instrumentalist view of education and of the pupils, one which situates the education system purely in the narrow context of serving the economic agenda of the state is certainly not one which is conducive to fostering a healthy educational environment in which the students can be esteemed in their own right. Finally, a culture which is overly dominated by the power of the market is not one which respects or encourages the freedom of the students. The freedom which is in theory accorded to each individual becomes in practice the freedom which money bestows. In this environment the economically disadvantaged end up having no freedom.

3. A PHILOSOPHY OR PHILOSOPHIES OF EDUCATION

At the outset of this paper it was observed that until very recently little attention had been given to the task of articulating a basic philosophy of education. It must, nevertheless, be acknowledged that in the extensive range of documents produced in recent years by the Curriculum and Examinations Board and the National Council for Curriculum Assessment there is to be found an impressive range of aims/principles of education which are presented as providing the basis for any curriculum reform. In addition, in two of the documents, namely, *Issues and Structures in Education* (1984)[18] and *A Guide to the Junior Certificate* (1989)[19] there is to be found a statement of the general aim of education. This is a particularly welcome reversal of an all too frequent trend to refuse the attempt to articulate a basic philosophy of education in favour of a pluralism of aims, a stance which is characteristic of a Wittgensteinian inspired philosophy of education and one whose pluralism is ultimately inseparable from extreme relativism.[20] What follows is an attempt, albeit brief firstly to examine the philosophical anthropology underlying the expression of this statement of the general aim of education and, secondly, to reflect on the overall coherence of the aims/principles through an examination of the references to 'cultural inheritance' and 'excellence'.

3. 1 The philosophical anthropology underlying A Statement of the General Aim of Education

In both *A Guide to the Junior Certificate* and *Issues and Structures in Education*, there is the following statement:

> The general aim of education is to contribute towards the development of all aspects of the individual, including aesthetic, creative, critical, cultural, emotional, intellectual, moral, physical, political, social and spiritual development for personal and family life, for working life, for living in the community and for leisure. [21]

By any standard that is an impressive catalogue of the multi-faceted character of human nature. It is also a much more comprehensive statement than that which is to be found in the opening paragraph of the United Kingdom Education Reform Act, 1988.[22] It is obviously intended to be more inclusive or all-embracing than similar lists of the dimensions of human personality which are to be found scattered throughout the other documents emanating from the Curriculum and Examinations Board[23] and the National Council for Curriculum Assessment[24].

Looking at it in more detail, the statement, apart from listing the diverse aspects of human nature, also puts forward, albeit in a slightly disjointed way, three broad goals to which human development is directed, i.e. personal life, family/community life and work/leisure. This is important because it recognizes that human beings are, by their very nature, ordered in terms of a purpose, goal or *télos*. It also recognizes that this goal, although it is weighted in favour of individualism, is not unmindful of the family and community dimension to human fulfilment.

However, there never has been a statement of the general aim of education that has been philosophically neutral and this one is no exception. How does one explain the place accorded in the statement to the reference to working life and the way it is distinguished from personal and family life? It is proposed as a goal to which education ought to be directed. Would it not be as appropriate, or even more appropriate, to see education or the development of the person (in the broad sense of that word) as the goal to which work ought to be directed, rather than *vice versa*? I am not denying the importance of work but it is a question of where one places the emphasis. The reason for the reference to leisure in this same context I can only surmise to be either designed to ameliorate the functional and/or utilitarian agenda suggested by the place assigned to work in this statement, or else, in a totally different context, it is designed to express the classical goal of *theoria* more properly translated by the idea of contemplation. If this is the sense in which the reference to leisure is intended to be seen, then it must be recognized that the classical philosopher who proposed the goal of *theoria*, namely Aristotle, saw the attainment of this goal as inseparable from the love of friendship. The lack of any reference to friendship sharply distinguishes this statement from any classical expression of the aim of education. Similarly the absence of any reference to dialogue, solidarity, the goal of naming or transforming the world, the lack of any social justice agenda distances this statement from contemporary philosophers of education such as Martin Buber and Paulo Freire who, from very different perspectives, emphasize the urgency of reaffirming in our contemporary world the essential interdependence of human beings. The emphasis on the development of the individual, despite references to family and community, place this philosophical statement in the context of Western liberal individualism. It may not be an example of individualism as extreme as the United Kingdom Education Reform Act which remarkably excludes any reference to family or community or even the social and/or political development of the individual[25] but it is still one which is weighted in favour of an individualism in which the economic or employment agenda is to the fore.

3.2 *Are aims/principles to be taken seriously?*
In the documents under consideration there is what is undoubtedly an impressive and highly extensive – almost too extensive list of aims and principles. For instance, it is questionable whether education can be seen as a preventative strategy in combating the

problems of vandalism, crime and drug abuse – something suggested in the *Programme for Action in Education*, 1984-87[26]. However, even when one looks at a more 'main-stream' educational aim such as promoting an appreciation of 'a cultural heritage' one is forced to ask the question whether it and, by implication, other aims are meant to be taken seriously. Under the broad heading of aims this ideal appears twice in the document *Senior Cycle : Development and Direction*[27] but when the document moves on to discuss that with which the senior cycle should be concerned there is no mention of the aim of fostering an understanding or appreciation of the students' cultural heritage. Furthermore, in the subsequent specific guide-lines for the transition year, leaving certificate or year six study programmes there is not the slightest reference as to how this ideal can be expressed through the curriculum. This is similarly the case in the document *Issues and Structures in Education* where cultural heritage is placed as one of four broad aspirations underlying the work of education[28] and appears nowhere else in the document. In the divisions of the junior cycle curriculum into a number of categories such as communication, language and literature, creative and aesthetic studies, etc. and in the subsequent detailed description of what these categories involve there is not a single reference to cultural heritage. I am obviously not saying that the omission is necessarily deliberate. Every education policy has its agenda but it is one which should be public and not disguised by 'pious' aspirations.

3.3 *Excellence or efficiency, or both.*

The former Minister for Education, Mary O'Rourke, in the article referred to at the beginning of this paper spoke of the importance that the Green Paper would attach to quality.[29] The ideal of excellence which is the goal to which quality aspires is undoubtedly a high priority. In two of the documents under consideration this ideal of excellence in education is highlighted. In the *Guide to the Junior Certificate* there is the following statement under the heading of curriculum principles:

> Quality: every young person should be challenged to achieve the highest possible standards of excellence, with due regard to different aptitudes and abilities and to international comparisons.[30]

In the document *Senior Cycle: Development and Direction* there is the claim:

> The board believes that the senior cycle must be sufficiently flexible and challenging to enable young people to achieve excellence in a dynamic and innovative society increasingly influenced by the demands of and the opportunities provided by new technologies, international trade and commerce and changing patterns of work, employment and leisure. [31]

There is no mistaking the 'economic' context in which excellence is discussed in the latter quotation. The former quotation is open to a broader interpretation. What both have in common is the linking of the idea of efficiency with that of excellence. In this they are faithful to the classical understanding of excellence. Only the one who aspired to excellence would ever be effective. The Greek word for excellence is *areté* ; it also means virtue. The Greeks recognized that only the virtuous person, the person of integrity, could be effective. To be effective, to be educated in any subject one had to be a person of integrity. In this expression of classical culture there was no artificial distinction between fact and value or between achievement and virtue. The two references to excellence in the passages above offer a fine vision of the importance of quality in education, but in the way in which excellence is defined in terms of efficiency rather than *vice versa* and in the absence of any reference to virtue or integrity it is a perspective which would certainly be alien to the Greeks. Our ability to recognize an ambiguity in the usage of the word 'clever' suggests that the neglect of the ethical dimension of excellence is not one which can be explained by ignorance.

4. PROPOSING A PHILOSOPHY OF EDUCATION :
A COUNTERBALANCE TO LIBERALISM

While recognizing the achievement of liberalism in promoting the virtue of tolerance and in stressing the equality and freedom of each individual I have, in the course of this paper, placed emphasis on the way in which the project of education can be distorted by the acceptance of scientific positivism, individualism, relativism and economic pragmatism. Given the influence of liberalism in today's culture, any statement of a basic educational philosophy ought to include a specific recognition of the interpersonal dimension of human nature; as a counterbalance to scientific positivism it should stress the cultural memory enshrined in tradition; and in opposition to both relativism and economic pragmatism it should include commitment to the classic ideal of excellence. In what follows I propose to limit myself to a brief treatment of the latter two motifs.

4.1   Education and a theory of the good: The classical ideal of excellence
The classical ideal of excellence or *areté* was founded on a belief in the objectivity of truth and value. In transcending the horizons of efficiency the Greeks proposed a theory of the good which recognized the essentially purposeful or teleological character of human nature. They also believed that in a community united by the love of the good it was possible both to know and to do the good. In contrast, the liberalism of our day was born out of the belief that it is not possible to know the good, that is, assuming there is a good to be known. Liberalism which is founded on this moral scepticism proposes itself as a philosophy which embraces pluralism but, as has been noted, it in fact canonizes utilitarianism or instrumentalism at the expense of pluralism. Times seem to have changed, but have they? The writings of Plato were the first systematic defence of the objectivity and transcendence of value and emerged precisely in the context of a struggle with Sophism – a philosophy which was based, like liberalism today, on a moral scepticism. There is, however, a difference between Sophism and liberalism. It lies in the fact that only the former has admitted that in the absence of a shared belief in the objectivity of value there is only one morality, namely, that of strength. Whether one phrases it in terms of 'the survival of the fittest', or 'might is right' the only imperative is that of power. In this sense the nihilism of Nietzsche's 'will to power' is the ultimate response to the pretence of liberalism that one can order a society harmoniously without any reference to a good or goal of human nature.

For the Sophist, education was a power game in which there were only winners and losers. Effectiveness was the name of the game, and excellence was only valuable to the extent that it was effective or efficient. Plato devoted his life to refuting this ideal of education. Prescinding from the inadequacies of Plato's own philosophy of education, the challenge facing educationalists today is to propose a theory of excellence which transcends pragmatic efficiency or examination competence. The alternative is to be resigned to an education system where counsellors and chaplains are employed for the primary purpose of providing *Band Aid* for the losers or the inefficient. It is not one to which we should aspire.

One cannot avoid the anthropological question. The challenge is to articulate a philosophy of education based on a view of the goal or purpose of human life. The difficulties facing those attempting to meet the challenge are formidable but not impossible provided a number of things are kept in mind:

> There is no neutral objective, ahistorical position from which to construct a theory of the good. Everyone is part of some tradition and consequently any articulation of a philosophy will inevitably be limited by the perspective of that tradition or history. This is not an admission of the inevitability of relativism but merely a reminder that, firstly, we do not have to aim at infallibility and, secondly, that any philosophy of education proposed must be open to criticism – it must recognize the tentative nature of its own formulation.
> No philosophy statement ought to be coercive. Insofar as possible it ought to respect individual autonomy. While not advocating an unrestricted pluralism it ought to be possible to frame a philosophy of education which respects diversity. Any philosophy statement should be framed in the context of a respect for basic human rights such as liberty and equality.

In the last analysis the value of a philosophy of education statement is that it enshrines a commitment to experience and understanding. In the language of the critical theorists it is the attempt to give expression to the ideal speech act – the force of the better argument.

77

4. 2. *Education and culture: Memory enshrined in tradition*

Education should include a moment of remembering. To the modern mind this Platonic perspective appears strange, almost unintelligible. It certainly would not have seemed strange to another classical, albeit late classical, writer, Augustine, who recognized that alongside the will and the intellect the human person can only exist to the extent that he/she possesses a memory. It is not just memory but more precisely it is time which defines us and what Augustine recognized is that there is an essential unity to time; there is neither present nor future for the person with no memory.[32] The modern liberal culture would have very little sympathy with this Augustinian perspective. As Heidegger (in the course of a work which was clearly influenced by Augustine) perceptively observed, our culture is defined in terms of forgetfulness or, more accurately, the refusal to remember. [33]

The rejection of memory or the belief in the irrelevance of tradition is what gives a coherence and a unity to the broad, diverse and sometimes ill-defined culture of liberalism.[34] Based on both the theoretical appeal of scientific rationality which renders any appeal to tradition redundant, and the historical emergence of liberalism in opposition to the authority or authoritarianism of tradition, liberalism today gives expression to the belief that the past is either dangerous or, at best, irrelevant and consequently life should be lived with as little reference to the past as possible. Those who value the past are labelled traditional/conservative as distinct from progressive/liberal. In this context the embracing of the cultural memory enshrined in tradition would be perceived as a form of escapism.

The reality is, of course, a little more complex. It is less than fifty years ago that Europe was traumatized by the holocaust. Given the ethical imperative 'never to forget' it is liberalism in its rejection of history which could be accused of escapism. The belief that we have nothing to learn from history or that we are not creatures of history reflects a blindness or a *naïveté* of a most dangerous kind.

Placing a value on memory is not to lock oneself into the past. On the contrary it is memory which shapes the questions which we ask of the future. It is memory that tells us that we are historical beings. Contemporary hermeneutical theory has done much to critique the ahistorical model of truth proposed by liberalism. In the course of this critique one of its most valuable contributions to philosophy has been to remind us of the fact that remembering is never the simple reproduction of something from the past. Rather it is always a new event – one that is inseparable from the exercise of human freedom and creative imagination.

Tradition speaks of the memory of a community, the memory of a culture. A desire to foster tradition or the heritage which is culture implies a respect for the untranslatable. Liberalism can have no regard for tradition because there is no sensitivity for the shared values, beliefs, ideals – for the shared memory or history which shapes both a community and the individuals who belong to a community. In addition, for the liberal, schooled in the confident belief that knowledge is equally accessible to all, irrespective of differences in cultural heritage, the idea that something is untranslatable is nonsense. We in Ireland have every reason to be wary of this liberal desire to create a type of cultural Esperanto, a world free of the awkwardness of cultural diversity. One does not have to have read the works of the playwright Brian Friel to be aware of the colonial agenda behind such an endeavour.

To place emphasis on the educational goal of promoting the cultural memory that is tradition is to recognize the importance of literacy. Too often the literacy problem is seen as that of functional literacy. Important as that is, what must not be lost sight of is the ever increasing danger today of the growth of a more corrosive cultural illiteracy – more corrosive because this form of blindness is not even acknowledged. The attempt to portray this concern with cultural literacy as a luxury which this age cannot afford is to fail to appreciate the seriousness of the issue. Having regard to the divisions in Irish society both North and South which are costing so many lives it is a priority which we do not have the luxury to ignore. Liberalism copes with division by ignoring the past. What is increasingly being recognized today is that it is only in the appreciation, rather than the denial of one's culture that one can acquire the resources to appreciate other rival and perhaps even incompatible traditions. History is not a series of answers, the history which one writes depends on the questions which one asks. Every culture asks the same but also different questions. It is only by being open to this reality that we can understand bias or prejudice. Liberalism has no real understanding of the roots of bias because it does not see that questions emerge from culture. It is therefore radically incapable of offering the possibility of conflict resolution. The contemporary 'critical theorists' have reminded us that the act of remembering or appropriating one's own tradition is never an act that is 'interest free' or neutral and that in consequence it is an activity which must be constantly open to self criticism. Liberalism, however, has no access to this activity of self-critical reflection. It is blind to the bias of its own tradition precisely because it does not recognize itself as a tradition.

The conclusion of this paper has been clearly signalled by the way my argument has been structured, an argument which inevitably reflects my own bias. The desire is for a statement of philosophy of education, one which expresses openly the understanding of education that underlies policy. It is the hidden agendas which undermine the possibility of real education. In any statement of a philosophy of education I would hope that the ideal of excellence, the importance of cultural heritage and the interpersonal character of human nature will receive their due recognition.

Notes:
1   *Irish Education: Decision Maker*, No. 3, (1991), p.1.
2   The following contributors to *Irish Education: Decision Maker*, No. 3, 1991 who advocated such a commitment include John Harris (formerly special advisor to successive Ministers for Education), p. 6; David Meredith (Secretary to the Church of Ireland General Synod Board of Education), p. 24; Br Anthony McDonnell (Provincial, St. Helen's Province, Christian Brothers), p. 26; T. J. Barrington (Chairman of the Advisory Committee on Local Government Re-organization), p. 10. An equally significant call for a philosophy of education can be found in Dermot A. Lane, *Catholic Education and the School*, (Veritas, 1991), pp. 10-15 and Donal Murray, *A Special Concern, the Philosophy of Education: A Christian Perspective*, (Veritas, 1991), pp. 4-6.

3   In the recently published book entitled *Irish Educational Policy:*
     Process and Substance edited by D. G. Mulcahy and Denis O'Sullivan,
     (Dublin: Institute of Public Administration, 1989), there is a
     sustained critique of the lack of scholarly analysis of the structures
     involved in establishing priorities for educational development in
     Ireland. In particular, Dr Denis O'Sullivan (ch. 8) argues that Irish
     educational policy is both localist and atheoretically issue-based,
     and that these characteristics in no small part contribute to what he
     describes as the impoverished state of Irish educational thought.

4   *Programme for Action in Education,* 1984-87 (Dublin: The Stationery
     Office, 1984), p. 1.

5   *Guide to the Junior Certificate,* (N. C. C. A., 1989), p. 12.

6   *The Curriculum at Junior Cycle:* A Position Paper, (N.C.C.A., June
     1991), p.2.

7   *The Curriculum at Senior Cycle:* A position Paper, (N.C.C.A., June
     1991),p. 3

8   *Sunday Tribune,* (6th October 1991), pp. 10-11.

9   Joseph Dunne, 'The Catholic School and Civil Society : Exploring the
     Tensions', in Conference of Major Religious Superiors, *The Catholic
     School in Contemporary Society* (Dublin: C.M.R.S., 1991).

10   *Irish Education: Decision Maker,* No. 3, (1991), p. 10.

11   K. Lynch, *The Hidden Curriculum: Reproduction in Education, a
     Reappraisal.* (London: The Falmer Press, 1989), esp. pp. 125-128. cf.
     also the article by Denis O'Sullivan of University College Cork in
     Decision Maker, No. 3, (1991), pp. 45-48.

12   Two authors who have highlighted the influence of liberalism on
     our contemporary culture are Alastair MacIntyre and Charles
     Taylor. Cf. Alastair MacIntyre, *After Virtue,* (Duckworth Press, 1981):
     Whose Justice? Which Rationality?, (Duckworth Press, 1988): Charles
     Taylor, *Sources of the Self: The Making of the Modern Identity,* (Cam-
     bridge University Press, 1989). Cf. especially pp. 495-521.

13   P. H. Hirst and R. S. Peters, *The Logic of Education* (Routledge &
     Kegan Paul, 1970). Note also the article by Paul Hirst, 'Morals,
     Religion and the Maintained School', *British Journal of Educational
     Studies,* 14, (1965-6) where Hirst asks (p. 7) 'What is the status of
     religious propositions? Is there here a domain of knowledge or
     simply one of beliefs?' He concludes that all we have is a domain of
     mere belief, and that, therefore, there is no justification for State-
     maintained schools to teach religion. The writings of P. H. Hirst are a
     reminder of the influence which logical positivism had on
     educational theory up until quite recently.

14 The writings of R. S. Peters offer the clearest illustration of the influence of 'Linguistic Analysis' on contemporary writings in philosophy of education. Cf. R. S. Peters 'Aims of Education – A Conceptual Enquiry' in R. S. Peters (ed.) *The Philosophy of Education*, (Oxford University Press, 1973); R. S. Peters, 'Philosophy of Education', in Paul H. Hirst (ed.) *Educational Theory and Its Foundation Disciplines*, (Routledge & Kegan Paul, 1983).

15 John Rawls, *A Theory of Justice*, (Oxford University Press, 1973), pp. 395-399.

16 D. F. Hannon and S. Shortall, *The Quality of Their Education: School Leavers' Views of Educational Objectives and Outcomes*, (E.S.R.I., 1991), pp. 189-208.

17 Leslie Bash and David Coulby, *The Education Reform Act: Competition and Control*, (Cassell Educational Limited, 1989), pp. 19-30.

18 *Issues and Structures in Education*, (C.E.B., 1984),

19 *A Guide to the Junior Certificate*, (N.C.C.A., 1989).

20 One of the foremost philosophers of education writing in the English language is R. S. Peters. Note his influential article 'Aim and Aims in Education', op. cit.

21 *A Guide to the Junior Certificate*, p.12 and *Issues and Structures in Education*, p. 14.

22 The Education Reform Act, 1988, part 1, chapter 1, par. 2, reads as follows: 'The curriculum for a maintained school satisfies the requirements of this section if it is a balanced and broadly based curriculum which:
(a) promotes the spiritual, moral, cultural, mental and physical development of pupils at the school and society; and
(b) prepares such pupils for the opportunities, responsibilities and experiences of adult life.'

23 The document from the C.E.B. entitled *Senior Cycle: Development and Direction*, (1986), contains the following statement: 'Senior cycle education programmes must be concerned with the personal, social and intellectual development of students.' (p. 14).

24 The position paper from the N.C.C.A. entitled *The Curriculum at Junior Cycle*, (June 1991), contains on p. 3 the statement of the general aim of education quoted above. The other position paper from the N.C.C.A. entitled *The Curriculum at Senior Cycle*, (June 1991), under the heading 'Principles of Senior Cycle Education' contains the following: 'Senior Cycle programmes should be distinguished by: (11) the centrality of the intellectual, moral, physical, social and spiritual development of each individual student.' (p. 9).

25 Op cit.

26 Cf. the commentary on The Programme for Action in Education 1984-87 by the Mater Dei Academic Staff in *The Furrow*, (October 1984), p. 640

27 *Senior Cycle: Development and Direction*, pp. 8, 16.

28 *Issues and Structures in Education*, p. 13.

29 Op. cit., p. 1.

30 Op. cit., p. 13.

31 Op. cit., p. 9.

32 Augustine, *The Confessions*, bk. 11, *On the Trinity*, bks. 9-15. For an excellent contemporary treatment of this theme cf. Paul Ricoeur, *Time and Narrative*, trans. Kathleen McLoughlin and David Pellauer, (University of Chicago Press, 1984).

33 Martin Heidegger, *Being and Time*, trans. J. MacQuarrie, (Oxford: Blackwell, 1973), p. 21.

34 The trenchant critique of liberalism contained in the writings of Alastair MacIntyre focuses on this feature of liberal philosophy. In particular cf. Alastair MacIntyre, *Whose Justice? Which Rationality*, (Duckworth Press, 1988), chaps. 17 and 18.

IV. Education and the Constitution

Gerry Whyte

The provisions of *Bunreacht na hÉireann* on education, like some constitutional Rip van Winkle, have lain dormant for the most part since their enactment in 1937. Drafted at a time when there was little or no demand for non-denominational education, these provisions reflected Roman Catholic social teaching by enshrining a principle of parental supremacy in respect of the education of children.[1] Operating now in a different type of society to that of the 1930s, this constitutional principle may have practical consequences which were never envisaged nor intended by the authors of the Constitution.

Two articles of the Constitution are germane to our discussion of education and the Constitution and these are set out here in full.

ARTICLE 42

1. The State acknowledges that the primary and natural educator of the child is the Family and guarantees to respect the inalienable right and duty of parents to provide, according to their means, for the religious and moral, intellectual, physical and social education of their children.

2. Parents shall be free to provide this education in their homes or in private schools or in schools recognised or established by the State.

3. 1. The State shall not oblige parents in violation of their conscience and lawful preference to send their children to schools established by the State, or to any particular type of school designated by the State.

2. The State shall, however, as guardian of the common good, require in view of actual conditions that the children receive a certain minimum education, moral, intellectual and social.

4. The State shall provide for free primary education and shall endeavour to supplement and give reasonable aid to private and corporate educational initiative, and, when the public good requires it, provide other educational facilities or institutions with due regard, however, for the rights of parents, especially in the matter of religious and moral formation.

5. In exceptional cases, where the parents for physical or moral reasons fail in their duty towards their children, the State as guardian of the common good, by appropriate means shall endeavour to supply the place of the parents, but always with due regard for the natural and imprescriptible rights of the child.

ARTICLE 44

1. The State acknowledges that the homage of public worship is due to Almighty God. It shall hold His Name in reverence, and shall respect and honour religion.

2. 1. Freedom of conscience and the free profession and practice of religion are, subject to public order and morality, guaranteed to every citizen.

   2. The State guarantees not to endow any religion.

3. The State shall not impose any disabilities or make any discrimination on the ground of religious profession, belief or status.

4. Legislation providing State aid for schools shall not discriminate between schools under the management of different religious denominations, nor be such as to affect prejudicially the right of any child to attend a school receiving public money without attending religious instruction at that school.

5. Every religious denomination shall have the right to manage its own affairs, own, acquire and administer property, movable and immovable, and maintain institutions for religious or charitable purposes.

6. The property of any religious denomination or any educational institution shall not be diverted save for necessary works of public utility and on payment of compensation.

Before embarking on an examination of the effect of the these provisions on the educational system, it is necessary to define our terms of reference. First, I have deliberately restricted my comments to the constitutional position of the functional family[2] in the provision of education and have deliberately excluded the impact of Art.42 on child custody disputes from my treatment of this topic. Thus I will not consider how disputes between parents as to the education of their children are resolved nor will I examine the power of the State to intervene in exceptional cases to remove a child from the custody of its parents.[3] Second, I do not propose to consider how the Constitution regards attempts by third parties to influence the education of a child not their own beyond noting that in two cases,[4] testamentary dispositions by such parties made conditional on the children in question being brought up in a specified religion were declared void against public policy because they defied the parental right and duty of education under Art.42. Third, in defining 'education' for the purpose of this paper, I see no reason to depart from the definition used by the Supreme Court in *Ryan v. Attorney General*,[5] viz. 'the teaching and training of a child to make the best possible use of his inherent and potential capacities, physical, mental and moral.' Finally, a comment about the nature of the right of parents, under Art.42, to provide for the education of their children, which is described therein as 'inalienable'. Explaining this term in the context of Art.41, where it also occurs, Mr. Justice Kenny said that it meant 'that which cannot be transferred or given away.'[6] However it should be noted that this description does not guarantee this right any pre-eminent role in the hierarchy of constitutional rights. [7]

1. THE POWER OF THE STATE TO PRESCRIBE A MINIMUM STANDARD OF EDUCATION
– THE SCHOOL ATTENDANCE BILL REFERENCE

Commenting on the general approach of the Irish judges to the interpretation of the Constitution during the 1940s, Chubb has written:

Judges tended to interpret the rights of the citizen conservatively, to give judgments that bestowed considerable powers and discretion on governments and to leave the extension of social and economic rights to the Oireachtas. [8]

This makes all the more striking, therefore, the decision of the Supreme Court to face down the Oireachtas over the question of education in 1943.[9] The School Attendance Bill 1942 proposed to oblige parents, on pain of the imposition of penalties,[10] to send their children within prescribed age limits to specified types of school unless, *inter alia*, it could be shown that the children were receiving 'suitable education within the meaning of this Act in a manner other than by attending a national school, a suitable school or a recognised school.'[11] Section 4 of the Bill defined 'suitable education' for this purpose as education, the content and manner of which had been certified by the Minister for Education as suitable. There is evidence to suggest that the underlying policy behind this section was twofold – to prevent parents sending their children to England to be educated and to ensure the teaching of Irish in all primary schools in the State[12] – and we may reasonably speculate that it was concern about the constitutionality of the first of these which led President Hyde to refer the constitutionality of section 4 of the Bill to the Supreme Court. [13]

The Court identified four constitutional defects in the power given to the Minister, by section 4, to define education as 'suitable'. First, the Court held that the Minister might require a higher standard of education than could properly be prescribed as a minimum standard under Art.42.3.2. Second, the Court took the view that the standard prescribed by the Minister under the legislation might vary from child to child, whereas that envisaged by the Constitution was one of general application. Third, the Bill omitted to empower the Minister to grant a certificate of suitable education in respect of a child prior to that child's sixth birthday. Given that some period of time would necessarily have to elapse before a certificate could issue, it followed that parents educating their children at home would invariably commit an offence in respect of the period between the date of the child's sixth birthday and the date of issue of the certificate. Finally, there was no constitutional warrant for allowing the Minister to prescribe the *manner*, as opposed to the content, of the minimum education required under Art.42.3.2.

Academic analysis of this decision has generally been critical[14] and it may prove to be of limited value in any attempt to anticipate the impact of the Constitution on contemporary proposals for educational reform. The basis for the first two objections has been undermined by subsequent judicial development of the presumption of constitutionality. In 1943, the Supreme Court understood this presumption to mean that

> where any particular law is not expressly prohibited and it is sought to establish that it is repugnant to the Constitution by reason of some implied prohibition or repugnancy, such repugnancy must be clearly established. [15]

In 1970, however, the Supreme Court extended this presumption to cover official acts authorised by legislation.[16] A clear statement of this principle can be seen in *Loftus v. Attorney General* wherein the Supreme Court said that,

> a statutory provision which has been enacted by the parliament established under the Constitution will ... be entitled, not only to a presumption of constitutionality, but also to a presumption that what is required, or allowed to be done, for the purpose of its implementation, will take place without breaching any of the requirements, express or implied, of the Constitution.

In the present context, this means that if the Minister for Education was given a discretion to prescribe the minimum suitable education which a child must receive, that discretion could not be exercised so as to stipulate a standard different to that envisaged by the Constitution. Furthermore, if the Minister attempted to exercise this discretion in an unconstitutional manner, the *application* of that discretionary power would be invalidated by the courts, but not the power itself. Thus Osborough concludes,

Mr Derrig, the Minister for Education who introduced the

Bill in 1942, can be counted unfortunate; it is by no means clear that the Bill, had it been brought forward today, would have met the same unpitiable fate. [18]

The third defect in the 1942 Bill identified by the Supreme Court was of a technical nature, which could easily be remedied by the simple expedient of allowing the Minister to evaluate the type of education being provided by the parents prior to the attainment by the child of its sixth birthday.

The fourth defect, however, warrants more detailed examination. According to the Court,

> [t]he State is entitled to require that children should receive a certain minimum education. So long as parents supply this general standard of education we are of opinion that the manner in which it is being given and received is *entirely* (emphasis added) a matter for parents and is not a matter in respect of which the State under the Constitution is entitled to interfere. [19]

This absolutist position was regarded by one commentator as providing

> effective protection for denominational schools as being the means chosen by parents for their children's education. [20]

More recently, a number of commentators have questioned whether the Constitution does, in fact, exclude the State from having any say in relation to the manner in which education is provided.[21] Essentially the argument is that content and manner of education are not separable and that any power to prescribe a minimum standard of education must necessarily encompass both content and method of education. Even if this is so, such a power on the part of the State is 'cabined, cribbed, confined' by the express constitutional rights and freedoms of parents. Thus parents must be free to provide this education at home or in private schools or in schools recognised or established by the State[22] and, in particular, they cannot be compelled to send their children to schools established or designated by the State.[23] Furthermore, in discharging its obligation to provide for free primary education and to attempt to assist other educational initiatives, the State must always have due regard to tbe rights of parents, especially in relation to religious and moral formation. That the State may regulate the manner of education in the interstices of these rights and freedoms is certainly arguable, but one wonders how extensive such a power can be. [24]

Thus the decision of the Supreme Court offers us very little guidance as to the extent of the State's powers to prescribe a minimum standard education. Quite apart from the fact that much of the decision has been overtaken by subsequent judicial development of constitutional principle, the Court's attempt at defining the 'certain minimum education' which the State could require under Art.42.3.2 was never very helpful. Counsel opposing the Bill had suggested that the minimum must be 'certain and precise'[25] and that it 'must be such as can be provided by parents according to their means.'[26] Neither formula was taken up by the Court which suggested instead that the phrase indicated 'a minimum standard of elementary education of general application',[27] a proposition which is scarcely enlightening.

One point about which we can be fairly definite is that the State's power to prescribe a minimum standard of education can only be exercised by the Oireachtas through legislation. Ironically, one of the side-effects of the Supreme Court's decision in the *School Attendance Bill reference* has been to inhibit the enactment of legislation, at least insofar as primary education is concerned. The unenviable distinction of being the first Government Department to lose a piece of legislation to the vagaries of judicial review presumably caused a loss of nerve within the Department which has yet to be overcome. [28]

2. THE STATE AND PRIMARY EDUCATION - *CROWLEY V. IRELAND*

Almost forty years were to elapse before the Supreme Court was again asked to consider the constitutional provisions relating to education. On this occasion, the subject matter of the litigation was not any legislative policy, but rather the manner in which the Irish National Teachers' Organisation [I.N.T.O.] had pursued an industrial dispute and the subsequent response on the part of the Department. The constitutional provision under consideration also differed from that in the *School Attendance Bill reference*, with the Court being asked to consider the State's obligation, under Art.42.4, to provide for free primary education.

In April 1976, a dispute over the appointment of a principal to Drimoleague National School led to an interruption of primary schooling for most children attending three schools in the parish. Prior to January 1978, the Department of Education had taken no steps to provide for primary education for these pupils, for fear, no doubt, of exacerbating the situation, but after that date it provided school buses to bring the children from the affected schools to other national schools in adjoining parishes.[29] In *Crowley v. Ireland*, a number of children, suing by their parents, subsequently brought legal proceedings against the State and the I.N.T.O. in which they sought, *inter alia*, an order directing the State to provide free primary education within the parish of Drimoleague. In the High Court, McMahon J. held that the state of affairs which obtained in the Drimoleague schools prior to January 1978 provided *prima facie* evidence from which one could infer a breach of the State's constitutional obligation under Art.42.4 to provide for free primary education and that the Minister had failed to displace this inference.[31] In respect of the period after January 1978, however, the judge ruled that, though the educational system provided by the State had to be reasonably accessible, there was no constitutional requirement that it must be located in the pupils' own parish; further, that the system of transport laid on by the Department did provide a reasonably accessible primary education for the children of Drimoleague and, finally, that such deficiencies as did exist in the education provided in this way did not justify the Court in saying that the children were not receiving primary education as ordinarily recognised.[32]

Confronted by the finding of liability in respect of the period to January 1978, the State appealed to the Supreme Court which, by a narrow majority,[33] reversed the decision of the lower court. Delivering the judgment of the majority, Mr. Justice Kenny emphasised that, by virtue of Art.42.2, the State was obliged to provide for free primary education but it was not obliged to educate.[34]

> The effect of [Art.42.4] is that the State is to provide the buildings, to pay the teachers who are under no contractual duty to it but to the manager or trustees, to provide means of transport to the school if this is necessary to avoid hardship, and to provide minimum standards. [35]

A significant implication of the distinction between the obligation to provide free primary education and the obligation to provide for it, and one which Mr. Justice Kenny spells out in his judgment, is that the Constitution endorses the existing system of primary school management.

> However, the State is under no obligation to educate. The history of Ireland in the 19th century shows how tenaciously the people resisted the idea of State schools. The Constitution must not be interpreted without reference to our history and to the conditions and intellectual climate of 1937 when almost all schools were under the control of a manager or of trustees who were not nominees of the State. That historical experience was one of the State providing financial assistance and prescribing courses to be followed at the schools; but the teachers, though paid by the State, were not employed by and could not be removed by it: this was the function of the manager of the school who was almost always a clergyman...Thus the enormous power which the control of education gives was denied to the State: there was interposed between the State and the child, the manager or the committee or the board of management. [36]

Turning to the facts of the instant case, Mr Justice Kenny agreed with the High Court that when free primary education had not been provided in an area for a considerable period, a *prima facie* inference could be raised of a failure by the State to carry out its constitutional obligation to provide for primary education. However, having regard to the evidence in the case, and in particular to the fear that Ministerial intervention in the dispute might have provoked a countrywide strike by the I.N.T.O., Mr. Justice Kenny concluded, perhaps surprisingly, that the Minister had successfully displaced this inference. [37]

The respondents had a further argument which was also rejected by the majority judgment. Counsel for the children had argued that, in addition to his obligations under Art.42.2, the Minister was also bound to defend and vindicate the children's right to be provided with free primary education under Art.40.3.1.[38] This provides:

> The State guarantees in its laws to respect, and as far as prac- ticable, by its laws to defend and vindicate the personal rights of the citizen.

In a passage which is less than convincing, Mr Justice Kenny stated that the obligation imposed on the State by Art.40.3

> is not a general obligation to defend and vindicate the per- sonal rights of the citizen. It is a duty to do so by its laws, for it is through laws and by-laws that the State expresses the will of the people, who are the ultimate authority. No sug- gestion has been made by the plaintiffs' counsel of a failure by the State by its laws to defend their rights, nor has there been any hint of the type of legislation which the State could have passed to provide for free primary education for the plaintiffs in Drimoleague between the 1st April, 1976, and the present.[39]

If, as appears to be the case, Mr. Justice Kenny is ruling that the ac- tions required of the State by Art.40.3 can only be provided through the medium of legislation, then, not only does that consti- tute a rather strange limitation on the efficacy of Art.40.3, it is ar- guably incorrect. The Irish version of this provision uses the word 'dlíthe' to describe 'laws', whereas one might have expected to see the word, 'reachtaíocht', had legislation been intended. Thus the plaintiffs' argument on this point may yet be more productively employed on some future occasion.

In summary, then, the majority judgment in *Crowley* provided a constitutional *imprimatur* for the inactivity of the Department of Education in the face of industrial action. However it is the reas- oning leading to this conclusion, rather than the specific conclus- ion itself, which is of more guidance to parties interested in what the Constitution has to say generally about the provision of free primary education. The distinction between providing for and providing such education, adopted unanimously by the Court, absolves the State from any constitutional obligation to establish State schools, though, of course, the State retains the power to establish such schools, should that be felt to be desirable.[40] Furthermore, it may yet be significant that the Court unanimously regarded that distinction as protecting the current arrangement of denominational control of primary education through the system of boards of management.

3. RELIGION, EDUCATION AND THE CONSTITUTION

In many ways, this is one of the more interesting aspects of our present discussion but it is also one of the most difficult. There are at least two reasons for this difficulty. First, the constitutional provisions relevant to this issue, and, in particular to the thorny question of State funding for denominational education, have received scarcely any examination by the courts in this context. Second, there is an internal tension within the Constitution itself on this matter, with some provisions justifying State support for denominational education, while others point towards a policy of State neutrality towards the financing of religion generally.[41] I propose to consider the two poles of this tension in turn and then investigate how the tension might be resolved.

Denominational Education and the Constitution: It is hardly surprising, given the history of Irish education, that a policy of State support for denominational education should be found in the Constitution. Thus Art. 42 explicitly recognises, *inter alia*, the constitutional right and duty of parents to provide for the religious education of their children and the freedom of parents to provide this education in private schools. Article 42.4 further obliges the State to

> endeavour to supplement and give reasonable aid to private and corporate educational initiative, and, when the public good requires it, provide other educational facilities or institutions with due regard, however, for the rights of parents, especially in the matter of religious and moral formation,

while Art.44.2.3 provides that

> [t]he State shall not impose any disabilities or make any discrimination on the ground of religious profession, belief or status.

It follows that parents are constitutionally free to send their children to denominational schools and should they do so, the State may assist such educational initiative, provided it draws no distinctions on the grounds of religious belief.

Finally, Art.44.4 explicitly recognises that legislation may provide State aid for schools, provided it does not discriminate between the different denominations, nor affect prejudically the right of a child attending such school to withdraw from religious instruction.

That provisions of this nature endorsed denominationally controlled education was accepted by the Supreme Court in *Crowley v. Ireland*[42] where every member of the Court subscribed to the view that the existing arrangements for the management of primary education along denominational lines were constitutionally valid.

However, in his book, *Church and State: Essays in Political Philosophy*,[43] Professor Clarke has argued that a system in which religious schools have a monopoly on the provision of education is unconstitutional for three reasons. First, it infringes the constitutional right of a child to freedom of conscience. In order fully to protect this freedom,

> parents, the State and other relevant authorities should protect the developing autonomy of the individual from the overpowering influences of religious indoctrination, in anticipation of freely made religious choices in later life. [44]

He continues,

> This is not an argument against religious schools. It is only an argument against a monopoly of religious schools. The constitutional rights of a minor to freedom of conscience can

only be protected and defended in an atmosphere in which alternatives to a rigorous religious tradition are made available, especially to young citizens. [45]

Whatever its strengths in the philosophical domain, this argument cannot be sustained in the context of Irish constitutional law for it fails to take proper account of the constitutional role given to parents in respect of the education of their children. The Constitution clearly recognises the authority of parents in this matter and, indeed, singles out for special mention, the parents' role in respect of religous and moral formation.[46] Professor Clarke attempts to counter this by arguing that

> the rights of parents cannot be appealed to as if they were the exclusive and decisive factor in arranging educational facilities for young citizens. Children also have rights, even if they are not aware of them, and even if they do not claim their rights in court. Therefore the Courts may constitutionally intervene to protect such rights, against the express wish of even a majority of parents. There is nothing strange in this conclusion; a majority of parents in a limited class are as liable to be wrong about the best interests of their children as, more generally, a majority of the electorate may be mistaken in supporting legislation which is unconstitutional. [47]

Accepting the validity of this argument, one still has to take into account the strong constitutional presumption that, in relation to the welfare of the child, the parents know best. A practical implication of this presumption, and one which is made explicit in Art. 42.5, is that it is only in exceptional cases that the State should take over the place of the parents in relation to the upbringing of children. Furthermore, it is fanciful in the extreme to imagine that the Irish courts, operating under a Constitution which obliges the State to respect and honour religion,[48] would share Professor Clarke's characterisation of religious education for children as a form of indoctrination, the deleterious effects of which necessitated State intervention in opposition to the wishes of the parents.

Professor Clarke's second argument focusses on the position of non-believers. He contends that the educational rights of children of non-believers, or of parents who, though themselves religious, are opposed to church schools, are currently frustrated by a policy of collusion between the churches and the State. Anticipating the argument that the rights of such children are protected by Art. 44.2.4, which guarantees the right of a child, attending a school in receipt of public money, to withdraw from religious instruction at that school, he submits that such a guarantee is useless in a context in which denominational schools are the only option available to the majority of students in the State.[49] An initial difficulty with this position would be the acceptance of Professor Clarke's contention that Art. 44.2.4 is insufficient constitutional protection for the rights of those who do not wish to receive religious education. However, even if one overlooks this difficulty, Professor Clarke's submission at best requires the State to support non-denominational schools for those parents who would wish to have such schools on the same terms as it currently provides for denominational schools.[50] It certainly does not require the State to withdraw funding from denominational schools for at that point the State would arguably fail to discharge its obligations under Art. 42.4. Furthermore the exclusion of denominational schools from public funding might also infringe Art. 44.2.2, which prohibits any discrimination on ground of religious profession, belief or status.

Professor Clarke's third argument is based on Art. 44.2.2 which prohibits State endowment of religion. He contends that this prohibition is incompatible with direct and indirect financing for religious schools at primary and secondary level and, at the third level, of a Roman Catholic seminary. [51]

There can be little doubt that the constitutional prohibition on State endowment of religion may have serious implications for certain aspects of current educational policy. However, in the light of the constitutional provisions supporting denominational education, it can hardly be argued that the State cannot finance denominational schools at all. But precisely what implications Art. 44.2.2 has for educational policy requires closer examination of this principle of non-endowment of religion and it is that to which I now turn.

Non-endowment of religion: Article 44.2.2 provides:
  The State guarantees not to endow any religion.

At the outset, it is important to stress that this constitutional principle has yet to receive any detailed consideration from the Irish courts. The matter surfaced briefly in *McGrath and Ó Ruairc v. Trustees of Maynooth College*[52] in which one member of the Supreme Court, Mr Justice Kenny, concluded that public funding for Maynooth College did not offend against Art. 44.2.2 because the College was not exclusively a seminary.[53] This matter was left open by Mr Justice Henchy and was not even considered by the remaining members of the Court. Consequently we must deal with this issue on the basis of first principles and must also bear in mind that arguments advanced here are necessarily speculative. As the Constitution is what the judges say it is, any authoritative account of this aspect of constitutional law must necessarily await a conclusive judicial consideration of the competing arguments heard in the context of actual litigation. [54]

The first fact of which we must take account is that, though the judges are the authoritative interpreters of the Constitution, there is no one authoritative method of interpreting this document. At least four different approaches to constitutional interpretation can be seen in the case-law.[55] We may call these the historical approach; the literal approach; the 'broad' or liberal approach (also known as the doctrine of harmonious interpretation); and the natural law approach. Applied to Art. 44.2.2, they offer a spectrum of legal propositions explaining the meaning of the principle of non-endowment.[56] I propose now to apply each of these approaches in turn (with the exception of the natural law approach) to the principle of non-endowment and then to evaluate specific aspects of current educational policy in the light of our conclusions.

The Literal Approach. The literal approach to constitutional interpretation demands that plain words be given their plain meaning, unless qualified or restricted by the Constitution itself. This is an appropriate point at which to consider the meaning of two specific words in Art. 44.2.2 – 'endow' and 'religion'. According to the Concise Oxford Dictionary, 'endow' means, in relation to an institution, 'bequeath or give permanent income to'. In 1944, this word was considered by the then Attorney General for Northern Ireland, J.C. McDermott K.C.[59] in an opinion replying to certain questions put to him by the Northern Ireland Ministry of Education concerning the effect of section 5 of the Government of Ireland Act 1920.[60] McDermott referred to a dictionary definition of 'endow' as 'to enrich with property; to provide ... a permanent income for a person, society or institution' and opined that it was in that sense that the word was employed in the 1920 Act. At the same time, he did not believe that every benefit connected in some way with a right or privilege over property would constitute an endowment, giving as an example, the use of a publicly-funded school for the purposes of religious instruction provided such religious user remained ancillary to the main purpose of the building. On the other hand, he did suggest that the payment of a teacher out of public funds for religious teaching would constitute indirect endowment of religion insofar as it would amount to providing regular income for the purpose of advancing religious education and, thus, some particular religion.

'Religion' is defined in the Concise Oxford Dictionary as 'particular system of faith and worship'. According to McDermott, this covered major world religions but also religions one within the other, e.g. the different denominations within Christianity. While Irish courts cannot, of course, be regarded as in any way bound by what McDermott had to say on these matters, one could not quibble if similar views were advanced as to the meaning of these words in the context of Art. 44.2.2.

Moving on to consider Art.44.2.2 in its totality, it may be regarded as a form of back-handed compliment to the ingenuity of lawyers that at least three different literal meanings of Art. 44.2.2 can be advanced. Let us begin with the least obvious of these. The use of the word 'any', it is argued, implies that this provision merely prohibits *discriminatory* endowment of any one religion over the others and that, provided the State acts equally towards all, it may, in fact, endow religion. Thus Graham, after comparing the language of section 5 of the Government of Ireland Act 1920 (which, in this specific context, is identical to Art. 44.2.2) with that of the First Amendment to the U.S. Constitution, which prohibits any 'law respecting an establishment of religion' argued:

> The language used in America, notably the absence of the indefinite article, suggests that it is a state involvement with religion itself which is barred, whereas in [the 1920 Act] it is a state involvement with one religion to the exclusion of others which is barred. [62]

The principal difficulty with this interpretation of the principle of non-endowment is precisely that it is not the most obvious meaning and that it places an excessive strain on the meaning of the words used. The practical implications of such an understanding of the principle also argue against its adoption. If the principle of non-endowment merely prohibits discriminatory endowment of religion, then the State is constitutionally obliged to fund all religions equally. While economists would fret about the consequences of such a proposition for the public finances, lawyers would worry about how to define terms such as 'religion' and 'equally'. Thus it is difficult to imagine the Irish courts adopting such a view of the principle of non-endowment.

A second literal meaning of Art. 44.2.2 is that it prohibits the State from providing any money to a religious body, irrespective of the purpose of the funding. The sense of this proposition is that, once it is established that a body has a religious purpose or dimension, the State is absolutely precluded from giving it any financial assistance.

Third, one could argue that Art. 44.2.2 only prohibits the State from financing the religious activities of religious bodies and that the State is free to provide money for the secular activities of such bodies.

However, as our formulation of the literal rule makes clear, plain words should only be given their plain meaning where they are not otherwise qualified or restricted by the Constitution itself. In actual fact, it is not possible to read Art. 44.2.2 in splendid isolation from the rest of the Constitution and consequently it is unlikely that either of the last two propositions correctly represent the principle of non-endowment. We must turn now to consider how the meaning of this principle is affected by its context.

The Broad Approach (Harmonious Interpretation) There are at least three other constitutional provisions which could colour one's view of the principle of non-endowment. These are Art. 42.4 and sub-sections 3 and 4 of Art. 44.2 which provide respectively:

> The State shall provide for free primary education and shall endeavour to supplement and give reasonable aid to private and corporate educational initiative, and, when the public good requires it, provide other educational facilities or institutions with due regard, however, for the rights of parents, especially in the matter of religious and moral formation.

> [t]he State shall not impose any disabilities or make any discrimination on the ground of religious profession, belief or status.

> Legislation providing State aid for schools shall not discriminate between schools under the management of different religious denominations, nor be such as to affect prejudicially the right of any child to attend a school receiving public money without attending religious instruction at that school.

Reading the principle of non-endowment in the light of these provisions, one can advance the following propositions as interpretations of Art. 44.2.2 which are arguably open to the courts.

First, the State is prohibited from providing any money to a religious body, except in such exceptional cases as are authorised by the Constitution and provided that there is no discrimination on the ground of religious profession, belief or status. In relation to this principle of non-discrimination, discrimination means a distinction either favourable or unfavourable in its effect on a person.[63] The principle is, however, subject to the qualification that such discrimination is permissible where it is necessary in order to implement or permit of the full and free exercise of freedom of religion.[64]

In fact, the only situation *expressly* provided for in the Constitution in which State aid can be given to religious bodies is in relation to education – Art. 44.2.4 – and here such aid is made conditional on there being no discrimination as between different religious denominations, no interference with the right of a child to withdraw from religious instruction at the school for which aid had been provided and, arguably, provision for such assistance being made by way of legislation.[65] One could also argue that Art. 42.4 implicitly authorises such subventions.

This general proposition is certainly open under the Constitution but whether it would be adopted by the courts is another matter. Such an approach necessarily precludes the State from providing assistance to religious bodies for non-educational purposes, such as, for example, the running of a hospital[66] and such a consequence might give the courts occasion to pause. A further point here, of course, is that even if this approach is preferred, it does not necessarily follow that the State has *carte blanche* to provide any assistance it wishes to denominational schools – one could still argue that the assistance referred to in Art. 42.4 and Art. 44.2.4 must be read in the light of the principle of non-endowment so that certain types of aid are prohibited.

The second proposition which one could advance to explain the principle of non-endowment is that the State may finance any secular activity of a religious body, provided, again, that there is no discrimination on the ground of religious profession, belief or status. This approach would restrict the scope of the principle of non-endowment to situations in which the funding would be used for religious purposes only. If this proposition is acceptable, then the purpose of the funding becomes all important and the State has to show that the funding is for a secular purpose, such as secular education or the provision of health services.

Again this is not to say that the Courts will necessarily adopt this proposition – one can see the argument that if the State finances the secular activities of a religious body, this frees up that body's other resources for religious purposes and thus the State may be endowing religion indirectly, which may be contrary to the principle of non-endowment. However one could argue that the principle of non-endowment should only prohibit direct endowment and, taking due note of the principle of non-discrimination under Art. 44.2.3, we can say that the proposition is open under the Constitution.

The Historical Approach This method of construction requires the courts to interpret the Constitution in the light of public opinion and the state of legal affairs as they existed in 1937. No less an authority than Mr Justice Brian Walsh, former doyen of the Supreme Court, has suggested in an extra-judicial comment that this would be an appropriate method of construing the principle of non-endowment.[67] In view of his influence on Irish constitutional law, it is worth setting out his remarks *in extenso*. After referring in a general way to Art. 42, he said,

> [T]here seems to be no objection to the State providing religious education, if the parents wish it for their children, and to the State providing the type of religious education requested by the parents. As taxpayers, parents should be free to require that some of their tax be devoted to the teaching of what they wish their children to learn. This is not a contravention of the provision in Article 44 whereby the State guarantees not 'to endow any religion'. The teaching of religion, or of any particular religion, as a subject in education is not be confused with the endowment of a religion. The United States constitutional jurisprudence, in relation to the constitutional bar upon the 'establishment' of any religion, has perhaps gone unnecessarily far in that, in effect, it has been construed as meaning that it is against the teaching of religion, or any particular manifestation of religion that might be regarded as the teaching of it.
>
> There are instances where historical factors are of some importance and should enter the consideration of the judges. The United States was particularly sensitive to the question of established religions, as indeed was the case in Ireland until the Church of Ireland was disestablished in 1869. But

the historical pattern in Ireland has been that schools have been confessional in the sense that religion of a particular denomination was taught in one school or another. No pupil was under any obligation to take religious instruction, and freguently in schools where there were children of different religions, separate provision was made for them. This is part of the social pattern of the country and would never have been, and is not, identified in the public mind in any way with the endowment of religion. It is a subject available in most schools, which the parents are free either to wish or not to wish their children to take. [68]

Such an approach to the principle of non-endowment would bring to centre-stage the state of educational policy and practice in 1937[69] and could obviously sustain some educational practices, such as the financing of religious instruction, which might otherwise be seen as contrary to the literal meaning of this principle. There are generally two objections raised to the adoption of the historical approach when interpreting a constitutional provision – first, that evidence of public opinion in 1937 on the provision in question is often lacking and, second, that such an approach fossilises the Constitution. There can hardly be any grounds for sustaining the first of these objections in the present context. However, as to whether the Supreme Court might be persuaded that this approach would fossilise the Constitution in an undesirable manner, only time, and the Supreme Court, can tell.

To summarise our position thus far, three propositions on State funding for religion would appear to be open under the Constitution – first, that the State is prohibited from providing any money to a religious body, except in such exceptional cases as are clearly authorised by the Constitution and provided that there is no discrimination on grounds of religious profession, belief, or status, except where such discrimination is necessary in order to guarantee freedom of religion; second, that the State can fund the secular activities of religious bodies, again, provided that in so doing, it respects this principle of non-discrimination; and, finally, that in deciding what is proscribed by the principle of non-endowment, one has to have regard to educational policy and practices in 1937. Various aspects of educational policy have been identified as problematic in this context. In particular, there is concern about the funding of Maynooth, the funding of teacher training colleges, the funding of chaplains in educational institutions, and what has been described as the 'permeation of religious values throughout the primary curriculum'[70] – the integrated curriculum. I propose to consider each of these under the three propositions referred to above.

If our first proposition correctly represents the constitutional position, then the funding of Maynooth and of the teacher training colleges can only be constitutionally justified if it falls within the scope of Art. 42.4. (Article 44.2.4 would not appear to be applicable here as such colleges are not 'schools'.[71]) It is not at all clear that Art. 42.4 necessarily protects such funding. It could be argued that the express saver, in Art. 42.4., of the rights of parents, particularly in respect of religious and moral formation, implies that that provision is only concerned with the provision of educational facilities for children and that it does not apply to third level institutions where the students are presumed to be sufficiently mature to take responsibility for themselves. Thus we would have to conclude that, under this proposition, there is some doubt about the constitutional propriety of funding these institutions.

They fare somewhat better under our second proposition, if only because here one could argue that these institutions, though denominationally controlled, are actually receiving State funding for secular purposes. If this argument could be sustained on the facts (a crucial issue which I do not attempt to prejudge here), then, provided there was no element of discrimination in the treatment of Maynooth and the teacher training colleges when compared with their secular equivalents, the allocation of public monies to such institutions would pass constitutional muster.

Similarly, if the Supreme Court decides to adopt an historical approach to the construction of the relevant constitutional provisions, it seems likely that the propriety of the funding of these institutions would be upheld, as such funding was an established aspect of educational policy in 1937.

I turn now to the question of public funding for chaplains. The function of a chaplain would seem to be essentially religious[73] and so, on the face of it, public funding of chaplaincy would appear to be an endowment of religion. If this is so, then, applying our first proposition, State funding of chaplains may not fall within either Art. 42.4 or Art. 44.2.4 as both provisions, interpreted in the light of the principle of non-endowment, would arguably not entitle the State to finance an exclusively religious purpose even within an educational context. Even if one could argue that chaplains fulfilled some secular purpose, one further constitutional issue would then have to be confronted in that, insofar as eligibility for such positions is restricted to persons of a particular religious status or belief, public funding of such positions would, on the face of it, appear to bring the State into conflict with its obligations under Art. 44.2.3 not to discriminate on the ground of religious profession, belief or status. However, because one's initial premise in this argument is that the chaplaincy fulfilled some secular purpose, it would not appear to be possible to say, as was said of analogous distinctions drawn in the College statutes of Maynooth in *McGrath and Ó Ruairc v. Trustees of Maynooth College*,[74] that this distinction was necessary to promote freedom of religion under Art. 44.2.1 – a veritable Catch 22 situation.

The same reasoning would appear to apply to the funding of chaplains considered in the light of our second proposition. Thus such funding could not be constitutionally sustained here if it was established that the chaplains fulfilled an essentially religious purpose, while if the chaplains discharge secular functions, the State would appear to be discriminating on the basis of religious profession, belief or status by endorsing a recruitment policy which excludes non-believers from consideration for such positions.

It is not entirely clear how the public funding of chaplains would fare under the historical approach to constitutional interpretation. As State funding of chaplaincy is a relatively recent phenomenon, one could argue that there is no basis for assuming that the People, in 1937, would have approved of such an arrangement and consequently no basis for applying the historical approach. On the other hand, one might argue that chaplaincy is but a refinement of a system of religious education which was in place in 1937 and, therefore, that it is constitutionally acceptable.

Finally, we turn to the permeation of religious values throughout the primary curriculum – the integrated curriculum.[75] This again is very problematic. Starting with our first proposition, we note that the two provisions which authorise the granting of State aid to denominational schools (or private and corporate educational initiative) both require the State not to trench on the rights of parents and children in relation to religious and moral formation and instruction. Thus, Art. 42.4 requires the State to have 'due regard ... for the rights of parents, especially in the matter of religious and moral formation', while Art. 44.2.4 provides that legislation providing State aid for schools should not 'affect prejudicially the right of any child to attend a school receiving public money without attending religious instruction at that school.' If religious instruction is integrated into the secular subjects of the school curriculum, then it would appear to be impossible for a child attending such a school to exercise his or her right to withdraw from religious instruction. Similarly it could be argued that the provision of funding for such schools does not pay due regard to the rights of those parents who do not wish their children to receive the religious and moral formation offered by the school.

Turning to our second proposition, it is again difficult to justify public funding for the integrated curriculum because the very fusing of secular and religious instruction deprives the curriculum of its secular nature. Consequently one is left with a situation in which the State is arguably providing a religious body with funding for a religious purpose, a state of affairs which contravenes this proposition.

Nor would this policy appear to be protected by the historical approach to constitutional interpretation. When the Constitution was enacted, religious instruction occupied a distinct part of the school day – Art. 44.2.4 arguably reflects this practice[76] – and thus one cannot argue that the very different system of religious education through the integrated curriculum formed part of the legal state of affairs or public opinion in 1937 which might influence one's understanding of the Constitution.

Non-denominational education and the Constitution: Before completing our account of the impact of the Constitution on the relationship between education and religion, it is perhaps worth listing briefly the constitutional rights and freedoms of those who do not wish to participate in denominational education.

First, and most specific of all, the Constitution guarantees the right of any child to withdraw from religious instruction at school without prejudicing his/her right to attend that school – Art. 44.2.4. Second, it guarantees freedom of conscience for parents and children – Art. 44.2 – and, furthermore, recognises the right of parents to provide for, *inter alia*, the religious and moral formation of their children – Art. 42.1 and Art. 42.4. Third, it enshrines a principle of non-discrimination on the ground of religious profession, belief or status – Art. 44.2.3.

Clearly, therefore, the State, and schools, must respect the right of the parents not to have their child provided with religious instruction and must do so by allowing the child to withdraw from the specific class of religious instruction.

Whether the State must treat non-denominational schools in exactly the same manner as schools managed by religious denominations is, perhaps, not quite so clear. Certainly one could argue that a principle of non-discrimination is implicit in the spirit, if not the letter, of Art. 44.2.2, prohibiting discrimination between schools under the management of different religious denominations in legislation providing State aid for schools. More to the point, one could argue that such a principle is required by the terms of Art. 44.2.3, forbidding discrimination on the ground of religious profession, belief or status. However, as we have already noted,[78] the courts read this particular constitutional prohibition in the light of the general guarantee of freedom of religion, so that distinctions or discriminations necessary for the full and free exercise of freedom of religion are constitutionally acceptable. *Quaere* whether one could argue that preferential State support for denominational schools is covered by this qualification.

Assuming that such a principle of non-discrimination as between denominational and non-denominational schools does exist, it is worth developing the implications of this principle in relation to the establishment of non-denominational schools. State aid for schools can, of course, be conditional and if the principle of non-discrimination applies, then clearly the same conditions for support must be applied to both denominational and non-denominational schools. Furthermore, and here one borrows from legal principles on discrimination law which have been developed in other contexts, it is arguable that if any such condition, which, on the face of it applies to both bodies, in fact places a disproportionate burden on one of the bodies when compared with the other, then such a condition will only be upheld if it can be objectively justified. To use a hypothetical example, if State aid was conditional on a school having a minimum number of 200 pupils, then such a condition might be more easily satisfied by denominational schools than their non-denominational counterparts, giving current attitudes and practices. But as such a condition would than bear more heavily on non-denominational schools, it would only be sustained if the State could point to some objective reason for retaining it, e.g. it might be argued that it would be an inefficient use of scarce resources to fund a school with less than 200 pupils. In this way, a balance is struck between the rights of the minority and the interests of the community and, again, the arbiters of this exercise will be the judiciary.

4. THE CONSTITUTIONAL NECESSITY FOR LEGISLATION

Penultimately, a somewhat technical point. By virtue of Art. 15.2.1, the sole and exclusive power of making laws for the State is vested in the Oireachtas. The Supreme Court has interpreted this to mean that the Oireachtas may only delegate parliamentary power for the purpose of implementing principles and policies previously adopted by the Oireachtas itself.[79] The dearth of legislation in this area, particularly in respect of primary education, and the consequent reliance on a system of administrative circulars emanating from the Department of Education may very well prove to contravene this principle. [80]

More specifically, in relation to education, it is also arguable that State aid for schools can only be provided for by way of legislation. Article 44.2.4 clearly refers to the provision of State aid for schools by *legislation* and arguably any other system of disbursement, such as by way of Ministerial circular, is not constitutionally valid, if only because it would not involve the same degree of parliamentary scrutiny as is required for legislation nor would it allow the President to exercise her power, under Art. 26, to refer the matter to the Supreme Court for an advisory opinion.

5. CONCLUSION

The constitutional provisions on education are, for the most part, an unknown quantity. Judicial precedents are scarce and, to a certain extent, unreliable. This is certainly the case with the decision of the Supreme Court in the *School Attendance Bill reference*, dealing with the State's power to prescribe a minimum standard of education, which has been largely overtaken by subsequent legal developments in constitutional law. Even the more recent decision in *Crowley* is primarily concerned with a pathological situation resulting from a trade dispute and may only be of limited value when considering the obligation of the State to provide for primary education generally. More significantly, the social context in which the provisions operate has changed dramatically since the enactment of the Constitution. The constitutional principle of parental supremacy was adopted at a time when the unquestioned premise was that parents supported the idea of denominational education. Thus the potential conflict within the Constitution between the policy of support for denominational education, on the one hand, and that of State neutrality towards the funding of religion generally, on the other, never materialised and the situation on the ground reflected the social teaching of the Roman Catholic church on education. More than fifty years later, however, that underlying premise of parental support for denominational education no longer holds to the same extent. Consequently the principle of parental supremacy may produce results not anticipated nor intended in 1937, especially in the area of State funding of education.

All of these factors make it very difficult to sketch the constitutional parameters within which an educational policy will have to operate. We know that the State may constitutionally prescribe a certain minimum standard of education which must be provided for children but we cannot define that standard; we know that the State, which is not obliged to educate, may support private educational initiative but we do not know to what extent. These questions, and more, must await a judicial ruling before definitive legal analysis of the constitutional provisions on education is possible.

Acknowledgement: I would like to thank the following friends and colleagues who assisted me with various aspects of this paper: Professor William Duncan, Professor Niall Osborough, Professor Una Ní Raifeartaigh, all of the Law School, Trinity College, and Father Paul Tighe, Holy Cross College, Clonliffe. Responsibility for any errors, omissions or opinions, however, remains mine.

Notes:
1   For a fascinating account of the drafting of the Constitution, see D. Keogh, 'The Irish Constitutional Revolution: An Analysis of the Making of the Constitution' in F. Litton (ed.) *The Constitution of Ireland 1937-87* (I.P.A., 1988).
2   By this I mean a family which is not in the throes of break-up. The Supreme Court has ruled, in the context of child custody disputes, that the family referred to in Arts. 41 and 42 is the family based on marriage – *State (Nicolaou) v, An Bord Uchtála* [1966] I.R. 567; *G. v. An Bord Uchtála* [1980] I.R. 32. It is inconceivable, however, that other families should be treated any differently in respect of the education of their children.
3   Readers interested in these issues are referred to J.M. Kelly, *The Irish Constitution* (2nd ed., Jurist Publications, 1984), pp.631-639 and the 1987 Supplement thereto, pp.188-189; J. Casey, *Constitutional Law in Ireland* (Sweet and Maxwell, 1987), pp.494-514; M. Ford, *Constitutional Law of Ireland* (Mercier Press, 1987), pp.583-589.
4   *Burke and O'Reilly v. Burke and Quail* [1951] I.R. 216; 84 *I.L.T.R.* 70; *In*

re Blake, decd. [1955] I.R. 69.

5   [1965] I.R. 294. For further discussion of some issues arising from this definition, see W.N. Osborough, 'Education in the Irish Law and Constitution' (1978) 13 *Irish Jurist* (n.s.) 145, at pp.169-171.

6   *Ryan v. Attorney General* [1965] I.R. 294 at 308. An attempt by Walsh J. to draw a distinction between inalienable rights that are absolutely inalienable and those that are relatively inalienable – *G. v. An Bord Uchtála* [1980] I.R. 32 at p.79 – has so far not found any support in the judgments of his brethern.

7   See *Murray v. Ireland* [1991] I.L.R.M. 465.

8   *The Politics of the Irish Constitution* (I.P.A., 1991), p.64.

9   This was the first occasion on which the Supreme Court struck down legislation passed by the Dáil and Seanad.

10   S.19.

11   S.3(2)(b).

12   See *Dáil Debates*, Vol.88, cols. 2094-8, 2111, 2122-23, 18 November 1942. Judicial hostility to both aspects of this policy was already revealed in cases like *In re Westby Minors* (No.2) [1934] I.R. 311 and *Carberry v. Yates* (1935) 69 I.L.T.R. 86. On the background to the 1942 Bill, see W.N. Osborough, loc. cit. at pp.174-180.

13   [1943] I.R. 334. By virtue of Art. 26 of the Constitution, the President may refer a bill to the Supreme Court for an opinion as to the constitutionality of all or any part of it. Should the Court hold that the bill is unconstitutional, the President must decline to sign it. In any other case, however, the President must sign the bill into law and, furthermore, the constitutionality of the measure can never again be challenged in legal proceedings – art. 34.3.3.

14   See W.N. Osborough, loc. cit.; J. Casey, op. cit. pp.519 - 521.

15   [1943] I.R. 334 at 344.

16   *East Donegal Co-Op. Ltd. v. Attorney General* [1970] I.R. 317; 104 I.L.T.R. 81.

17   [1979] I.R. 221.

18   Loc. cit. at p.174.

19   [1943] I.R. 334 at 344.

20   V. Grogan, 'Schools under the Constitution' (1970) *Studies* 377, at p.378.

21   See J. Casey, op. cit. at p.520; W.N. Osborough, loc. cit. at p.173.

22   Art. 42.2.

23   Art. 42.3.1. This provision reads: 'The State shall not oblige parents in violation of their conscience and lawful preference to send their children to schools established by the State, or to any particular type of school designated by the State.' In the *School Attendance Bill*

reference, the Supreme Court noted the argument that s.3 of the Bill might also have been unconstitutional because it merely recognised religious grounds as a reason for not sending a child to a designated school, while Art. 42.3.1 referred to the broader ground of violation of conscience and lawful preference. However as the Court had been requested to consider the constitutionality of s.4 only, it did not have to rule on this issue.

24   Commenting on one aspect of this topic, the role of State schools, Alvey says, 'The establishment of State schools is not banned under the Constitution, but there seems to be a constitutional bias against their establishment, as though they should be established only by default of the denominational authorities', and, later, 'Overall, there seems to be no grounds for forcing the State, through appeals to the Constitution, to provide schools that are not denominational.' *Irish Education – the case for secular reform* (Church and State Books, 1991) at pp.84,85. Though on this latter point, see above, pp. 107-108.

25   [1943] I.R. 334 at 337.

26   Ibid. at 338.

27   Ibid. at 345.

28   See below, pp. 109-110. The 1967 Report of the Committee on the Constitution (Pr.9817) recommended, at para.133, that the difficulties posed by this decision be overcome by the replacement of Art. 42.3.2 with a provision along the following lines – 'Laws, however, may be enacted to oblige parents who have failed in their duty to provide for the education of their children to send their children to schools established or designated by the State.' Nothing came of this proposal.

29   The provision of these buses had initially been ordered by the High Court in December 1977 as a temporary solution but this arrangement was continued in place under the terms of a compromise worked out between the parties.

30   [1980] I.R. 102. The plaintiffs' claim against the I.N.T.O. for damages for interference with constitutional rights was held to have been made out and led to a number of subsequent cases against the union, see *Hayes v. Ireland* [1987] I.L.R.M. 651; *Conway v. I.N.T.O.* [1991] I.L.R.M. 497; *Hurley v. I.N.T.O.*, Supreme Court, 14 February 1991; *Sheehan v. I.N.T.O.* Supreme Court, 14 February 1991. The implications of this decision for unions engaging in industrial action are potentially very serious but, in the context of the present discussion, need not detain us further.

31   A curious feature of this judgment is that McMahon J. himself says that the plaintiffs' claim only concerned the period after January

1978 – see p.112 of the report – and yet he proceeded to rule on the State's liability prior to that time. The implication that he may have exceeded his brief was not taken up in the subsequent appeal to the Supreme Court.

32   By implication, the State could be held liable for failing to provide for primary education if the deficiencies in the system were of the appropriate magnitude. Yet in the *School Attendance Bill reference*, the Supreme Court ruled that the State had no authority whatsoever to prescribe the appropriate manner in which the constitutionally prescribed minimum education was to be provided – a clear case of responsibility without power.

33   Mr Justices Kenny, Henchy and Griffin were in the majority, while the Chief Justice, Mr Justice O'Higgins and Mr Justice Parke dissented.

34   The Court distinguished between the obligation to provide for education and the obligation to provide education. The sense of this distinction is perhaps more apparent in the Irish text of the Constitution which translates the parent's right 'to provide for' education in Art. 42.1 as 'oideachas … a chur ar fáil' while the same phrase used in relation to the State in Art. 42.4 is 'socrú a dhéanamh chun bunoideachas a bheith ar fáil.'

35   [1980] I.R. 102 at 126.

36   Ibid. at 126-7. See, to similar effect, the following passage in the dissenting judgment of the Chief Justice, Mr Justice O'Higgins at p.122 of the report – '[Art.42.4] was intended to avoid imposing a mandatory obligation on the State directly to provide free primary education. Such, if imposed, might have led to the provision of free primary education in exclusively State schools. Rather was it intended that the State should ensure by the arrangements it made that free primary education would be provided. When one remembers the long and turbulent history of the church schools in Ireland, and the sustained struggle for the right to maintain such schools by the religious authorities of all denominations in all parts of Ireland, one can well understand the care with which the words used must have been selected.'

37   It was on this point that the dissenting judges parted company with their brethern, the Chief Justice, Mr Justice O'Higgins (with whom Mr Justice Parke concurred) taking the view that, even prior to the introduction of the transport system in January 1978, the Minister had an obligation to try to help the children locally in Drimoleague itself. For academic support of this dissent, see J. Casey, op. cit. pp.518-9.

38 This provision is the source of constitutional protection for unenumerated constitutional rights – see *Ryan v. Attorney General* [1965] I.R. 294.

39 [1980] I.R. 102 at 130.

40 Arts. 42.2 and 42.3.1 clearly recognise the legitimacy of such a power.

41 In this, however, the *Bunreacht* is no different from two earlier constitutional documents of this century – the Government of Ireland Act 1920 and the Constitution of the Irish Free State, 1922. Thus, s.5 of the former forbade the Parliaments of Southern and Northern Ireland from making a law 'so as either directly or indirectly to establish or endow any religion … or affect prejudically the right of any child to attend a school receiving public money without attending the religious instruction at that school.' A clear implication of the second limb of this provision is that public monies could be given to schools providing religious education. Subsequently, art. 8 of the Constitution of the Irish Free State provided that 'no law may be made either directly or indirectly to endow any religion… or affect prejudically the right of any child to attend a school receiving public money without attending the religious instruction at the school, or make any discrimination as respects State aid between schools under the management of different religious denominations.'

42 [1980] I.R. 102. See above, p. 92.

43 Cork University Press, 1984.

44 Ibid., p.219.

45 Ibid. The validity of this disclaimer is difficult to accept for, if Professor Clarke's basic thesis is correct, then the existence of only one school providing 'religious indoctrination' would infringe the constitutional freedoms of its own pupils.

46 Art. 42.2.

47 Op. cit. p.209.

48 Art. 44.1.

49 Op. cit. at p.222. One could also pray in aid, in support of the rights of such families, Art.42.4 which expressly recognises the rights of parents in the matter of religious and moral formation and which, one assumes, protects the rights of non-believers as much as believers; Art. 42.2 which guarantees the freedom of parents to provide such education, *inter alia*, at home or in private schools, including, presumably, non-denominational schools; and, more generally, Art. 44.2.1, guaranteeing freedom of conscience. But presumably these arguments would also be covered by Professor Clarke's rebuttal of the argument based on Art. 44.2.4.

50 For further examination of this proposition, see above, pp. 108-109.

51 Op. cit., p.222 et seq.

52   [1979] I.L.R.M. 166.
53   Casey, however, is of the opinion that public funding for Maynooth does contravene Art. 44.2.2 – op. cit., pp.560-1. See below, pp. 105-106 of this text. This issue is complicated by the fact that Maynooth is, at the one time, a seminary, a Pontifical University and a recognised college of the National University of Ireland.
54   Though this may not be long in coming, for litigation is currently in train on the propriety of State funding for school chaplains and for the integrated curriculum. See D. Alvey, op. cit. p.85. 55 For an excellent account of this area, see G. Hogan, 'Constitutional Interpretation' in F. Litton (ed.), *The Constitution of Ireland 1937-87* (I.P.A., 1988), p.173.
56   Hogan comments, loc. cit., p.187, '[N]o particular theory or method of constitutional interpretation has been applied by the courts. Indeed, this lack of consistency has been so prevalent that individual judges have from time to time adopted different approaches to this question, utilising whatever method might seem to be most convenient or to offer adventitious support for conclusions they had already reached.'
57   The author is not aware of any principle of natural law which would have a bearing on the meaning of this principle of non-endowment.
58   Ó Donaill, *Foclóir Gaeilge-Béarla* (1977), renders the equivalent word in the Irish text of the Constitution, 'maoinigh', simply as 'finance, endow'.
59   Who subsequently became Lord Chief Justice of Northern Ireland.
60   This opinion is set out in full in the appendix to an article by Edgar Graham, 'Religion and Education – The Constitutional Problem' (1982) 33 N.I.L.Q. 20.
61   Ó Donaill defines 'creideamh' as 'belief, faith; religion, creed', so the equivalent Irish phrase in Art. 44.2.2 – 'córas creidimh' translates variously as 'system of belief or faith or religion or creed.'
62   Graham, loc. cit., p.35.
63   See *Quinn's Supermarket Ltd. v. Attorney General* [1972] I.R. 1.
64   This judicial gloss on the terms of Art. 44.2.3 is contained in the Supreme Court judgment in *Mulloy v. Minister for Education* [1975] I.R. 88 (at 96) and in the judgment of Mr Justice Henchy in the Supreme Court decision in *McGrath and Ó Ruairc v. Trustees of Maynooth College* [1979] I.L.R.M. 166 (at 187).
65   See further above, pp. 109-110.
66   According to Casey, it is not clear whether public financing of denominationally controlled hospitals is consonant with the principle of non-endowment – op. cit., pp. 558-9.

67 See 'The Constitution and Constitutional Rights' in *The Constitution of Ireland 1937-1987*, ed. F. Litton, (I.P.A., 1988) at p.86. This approach was also used by Mr Justice Kenny in *Crowley v. Ireland* [1980] I.R. 102. See above, p. 92.

68 Ibid., pp. 99-100. Judge Walsh then proceeded to suggest, though not on the basis of this historical approach to constitutional interpretation, that some accommodation must be made for the teacher who conscientiously objects to having to teach religion. However he does not appear to consider a teacher's non-belief in religion *per se* as affording such a person a conscientious objection in this context.

69 On the history of Irish education, see J. Coolahan, *Irish Education: Its History and Structure* (Dublin, 1981).

70 D. Alvey, op. cit ., p. 85 .

71 See J. Casey, op. cit., p. 560.

72 On the introduction of State funding for Protestant teacher training colleges, see Ó Ceallaigh, 'Disestablishment and Church Education' (1970) 10 *Studica Hibernica* 36.

73 This proposition is based on the premise that chaplains are invariably ordained or professed or active lay members of a Church.

74 [1979] I.L.R.M. 166. An essential difference between the *Maynooth* case and the question of public funding of chaplains is that, in the former, the Supreme Court did not, on the facts of the case, have to consider the principle of non-endowment.

75 For the sake of the discussion, I am prepared to assume that such values do permeate the curriculum and that this constitutes a form of religious instruction. However whether this assumption is factually correct I am not professionally competent to say.

76 Mr Justice Walsh's comments on the freedom of the State to finance religious education – quoted above at p. 103-104 – are arguably informed by a similar understanding of the method of instruction.

77 See above, p. 101.

78 See above, p. 101 of this text.

79 *Cityview Press Ltd. v. An Chomhairle Oiliúna* [1980] I.R. 381.

80 This problem has already been adverted to by W.N. Osborough, loc. cit., p.174; J. Casey, op. cit. , p.251 and D. Alvey, op. cit. pp.86-87. Alvey also draws attention to the position of comprehensive and community schools in this regard.

Contributors

JOHN M. HULL is Professor of Religious Education and Dean of the Faculty of Education and Continuing Studies in the University of Birmingham. His autobiography, *Touching the Rock: an Experience of Blindness*, London, Arrow Books, 1991, has been translated into several languages.

KEVIN WILLIAMS is a full time lecturer in the Education Department of Mater Dei Institute. He has published widely on educational and philosophical issues in Irish and international journals.

EOIN CASSIDY is a priest of the Archdiocese of Dublin. He is Head of the Philosphy Department at Mater Dei Institute and also teaches Philosophy in Holy Cross College, Clonliffe.

GERRY WHYTE, a law lecturer and fellow of Trinity College, Dublin, is co-author of the 1987 Supplement to J.M. Kelly's *The Irish Constitution*. He is the current vice-chairperson of the Irish Commission for Justice and Peace.

DERMOT A. LANE is a priest of the Archdiocese of Dublin and Director of Studies at Mater Dei Institute. He recently published a pamphlet entitled *Catholic Education and the School: Some Theological Reflections*, Veritas, 1991.